Women of the Grand Theater

Posters of the Glamourous Women of the Early 20th Century

By, Patrick W. Nee

~Grand Posters of the Past™~

World Great Art™ Publishing

www.WorldGreatArt.com

World Great Art™ Publishing

Published by:

World Great Art Publishing

96 Walter Street/ Suite 200

Boston, MA 02131, USA

Tel: 617-354-7722

www.WorldGreatArt.com

For ordering posters of prints, contact manager@worldgreatart.com

World Great Art™ Publishing

www.WorldGreatArt.com

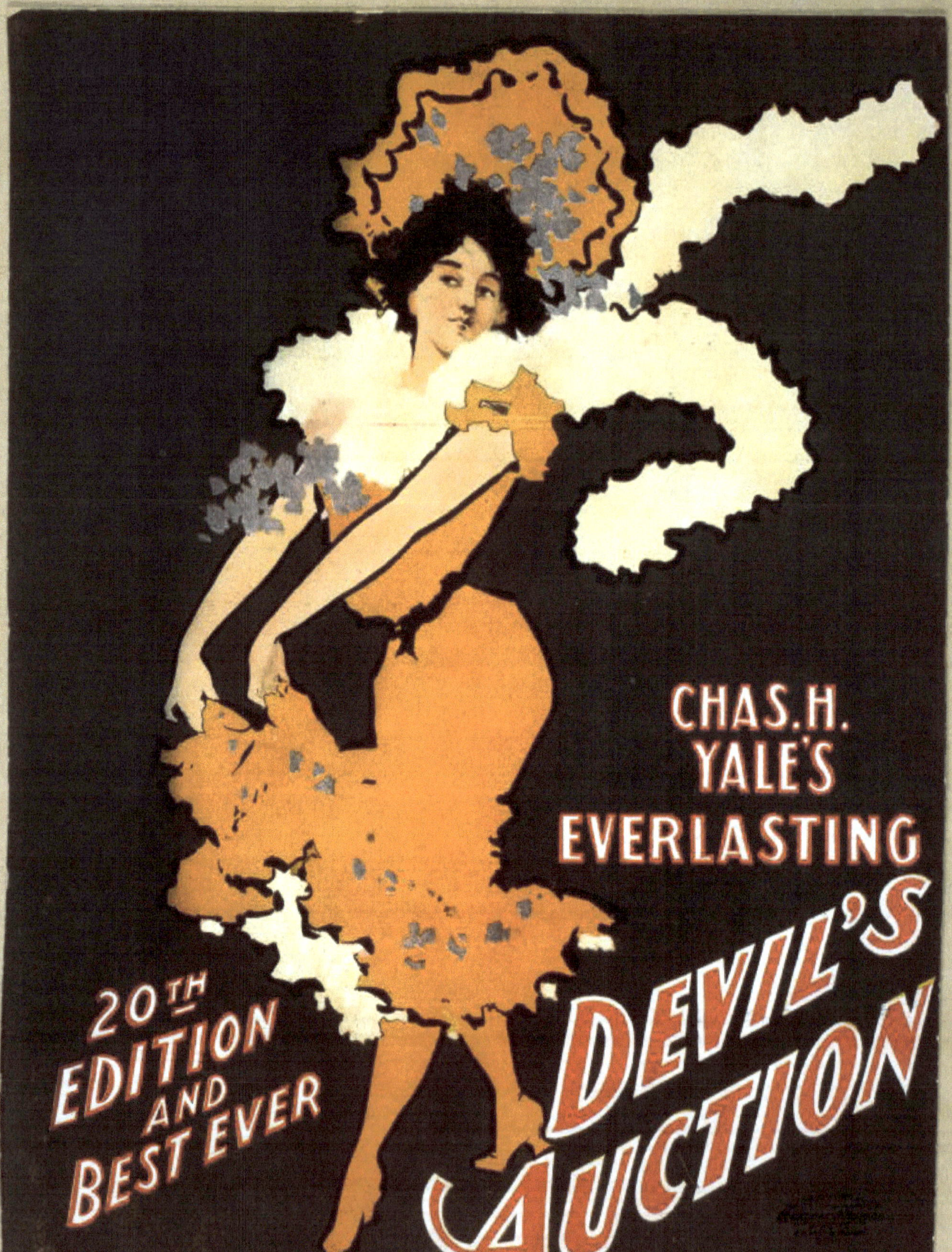
CHAS. H.
YALE'S
EVERLASTING
DEVIL'S
AUCTION
20TH
EDITION
AND
BEST EVER

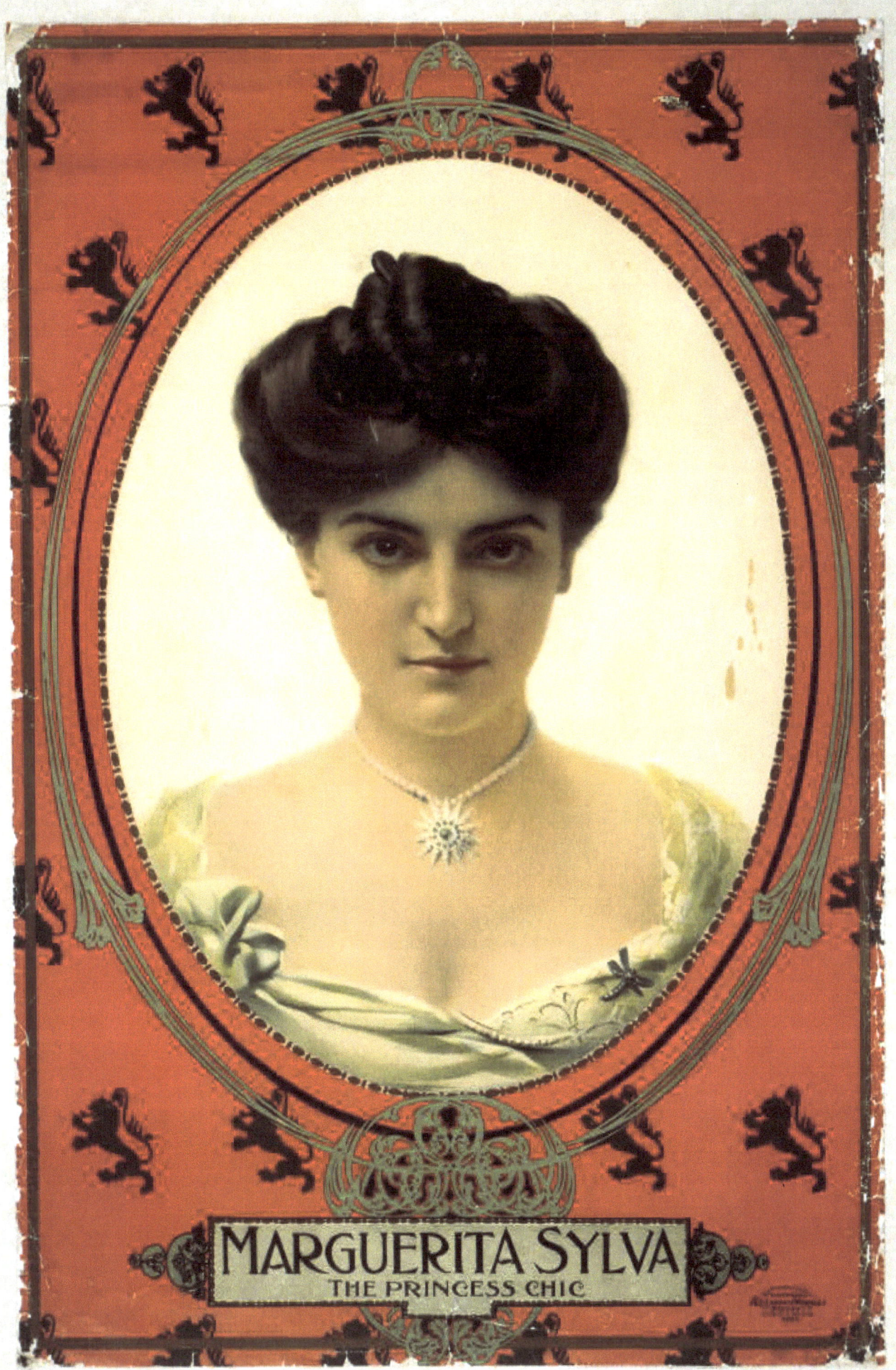

MARGUERITA SYLVA

THE PRINCESS CHIC

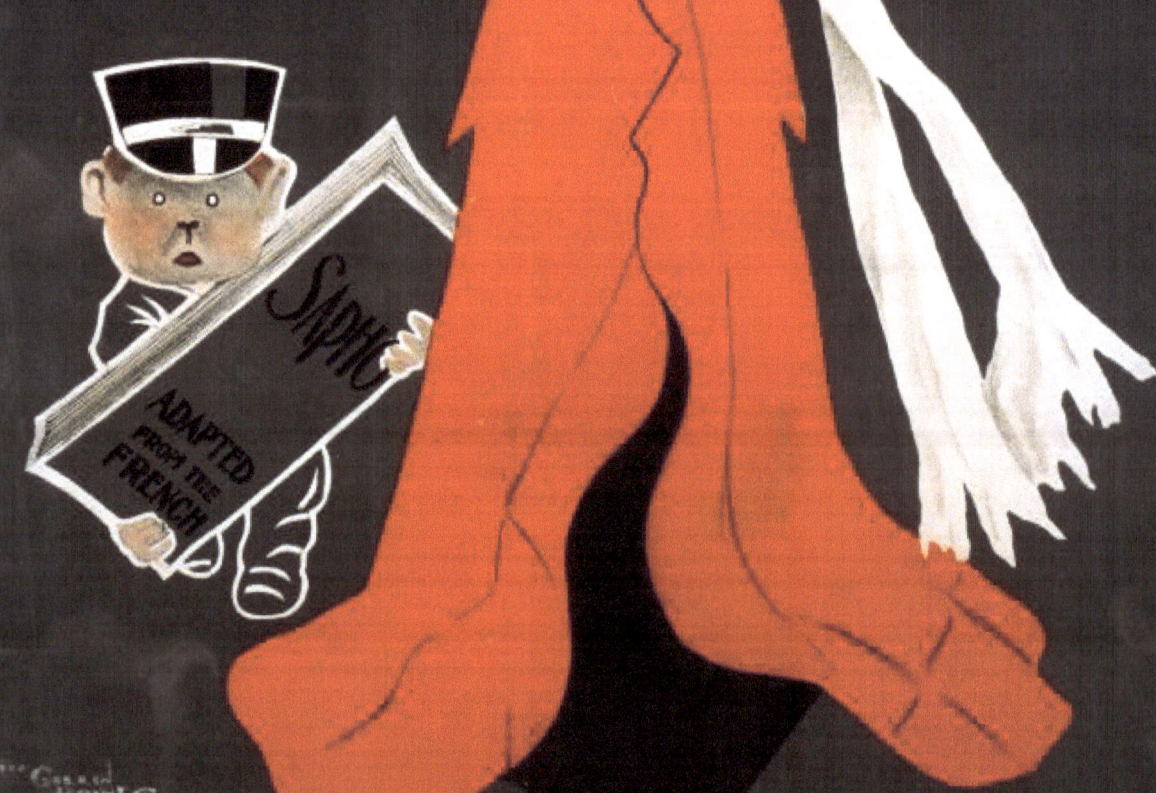

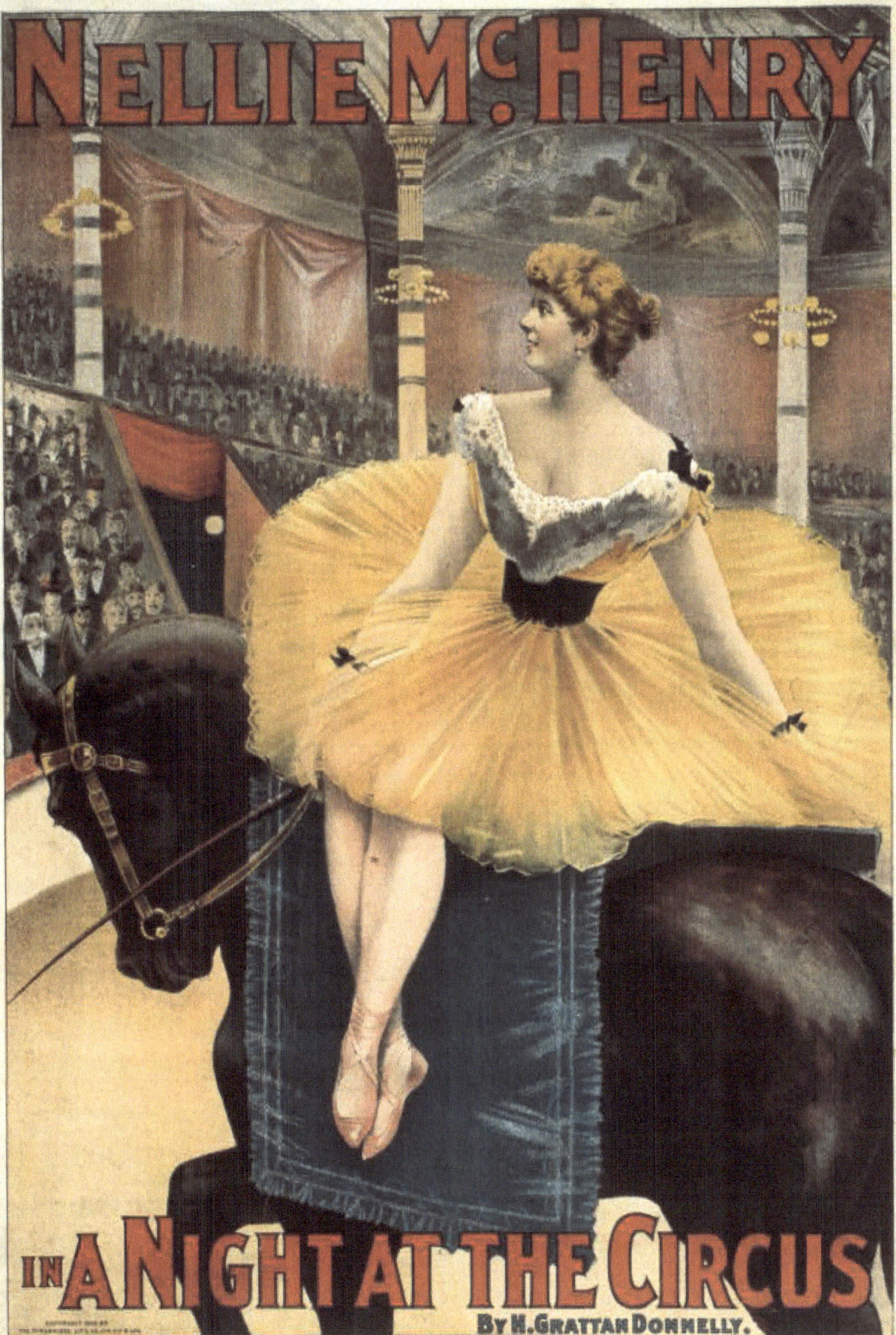

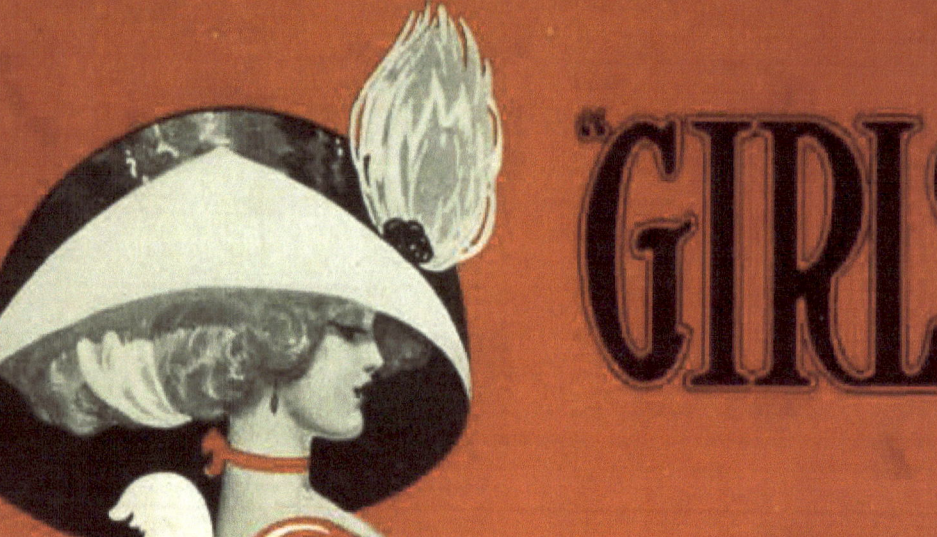

CLYDE FITCH'S
GREATEST COMEDY

"GIRLS"

MISS VIOLET

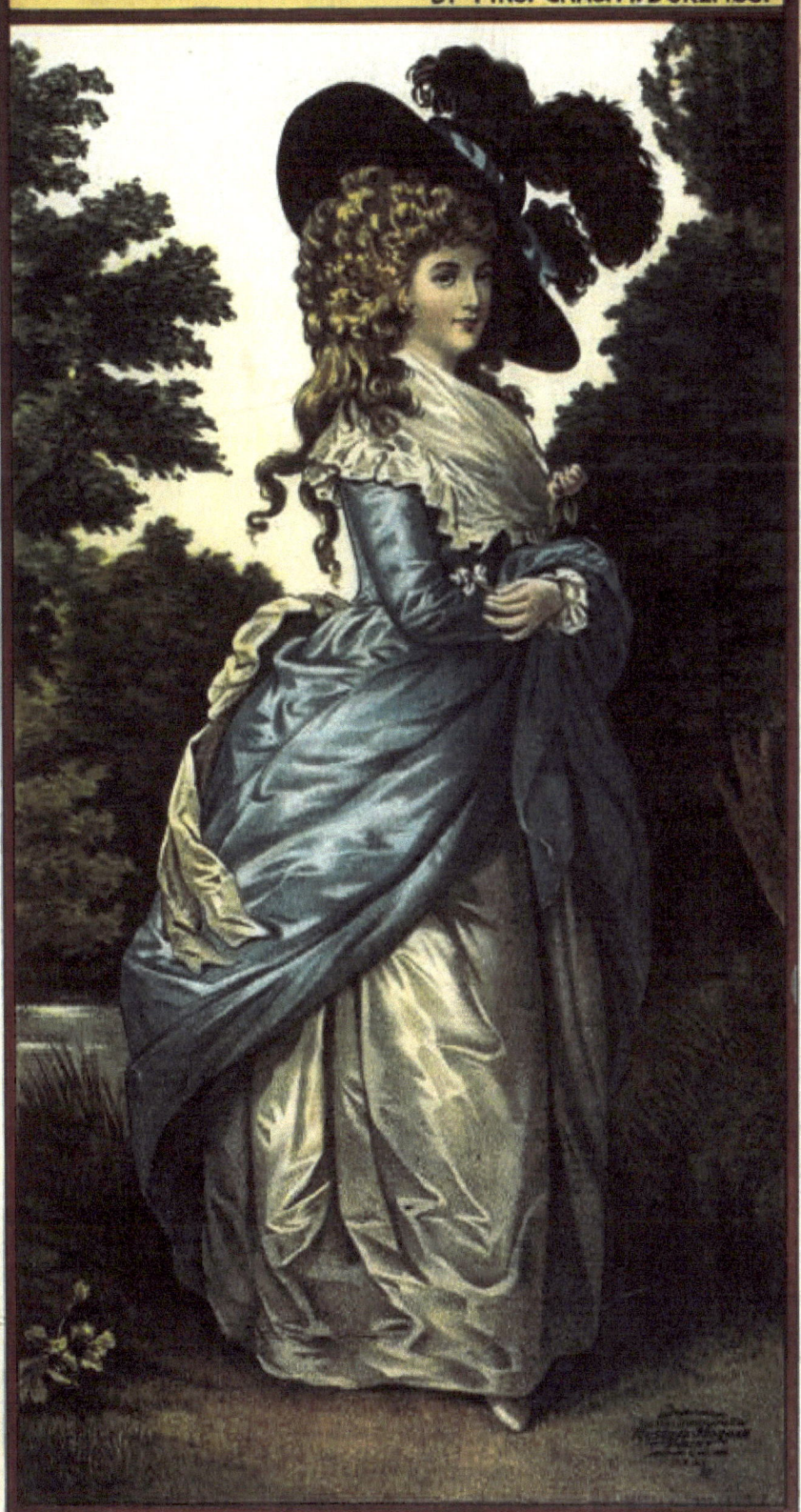

SWEELY, SHIPMAN & CO. PRESENT
THE DUCHESS OF DEVONSHIRE
BY MRS. CHAS. A. DOREMUS.

Silver Spur.

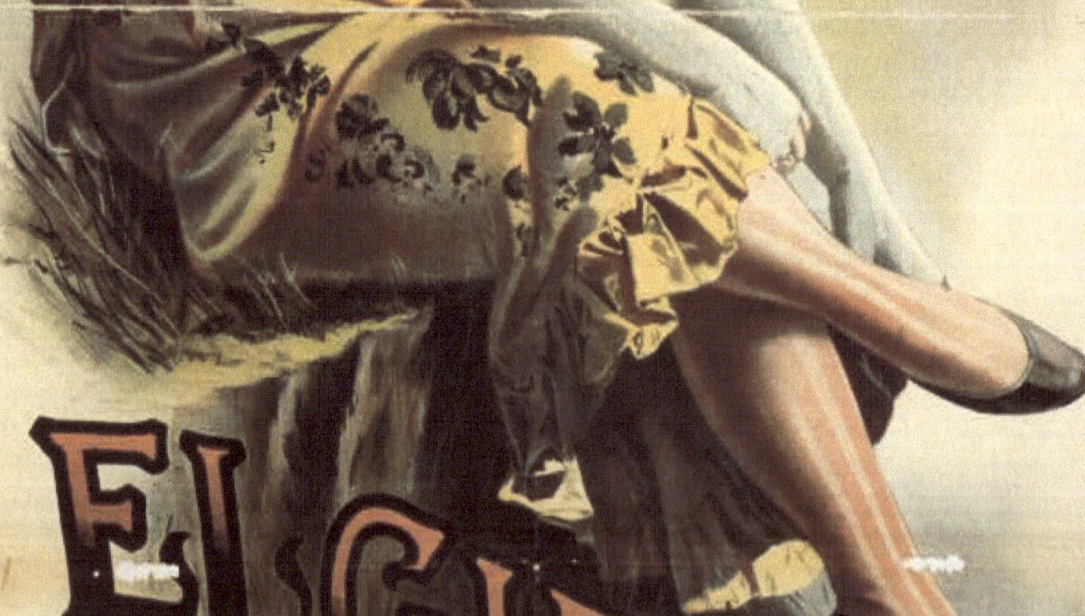

ELGIE.

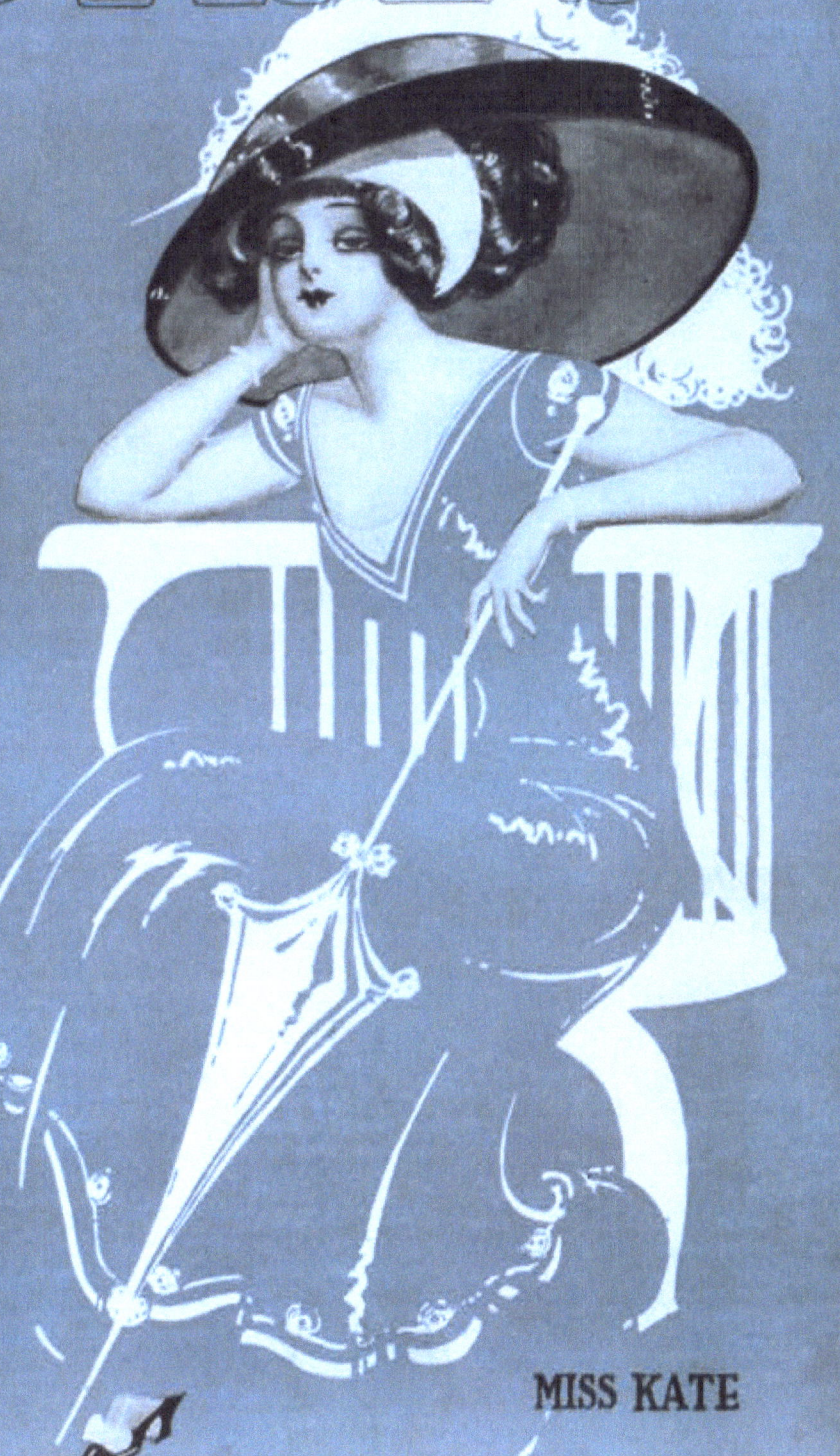

CLYDE FITCH'S
GREATEST COMEDY
"GIRLS"

MISS KATE

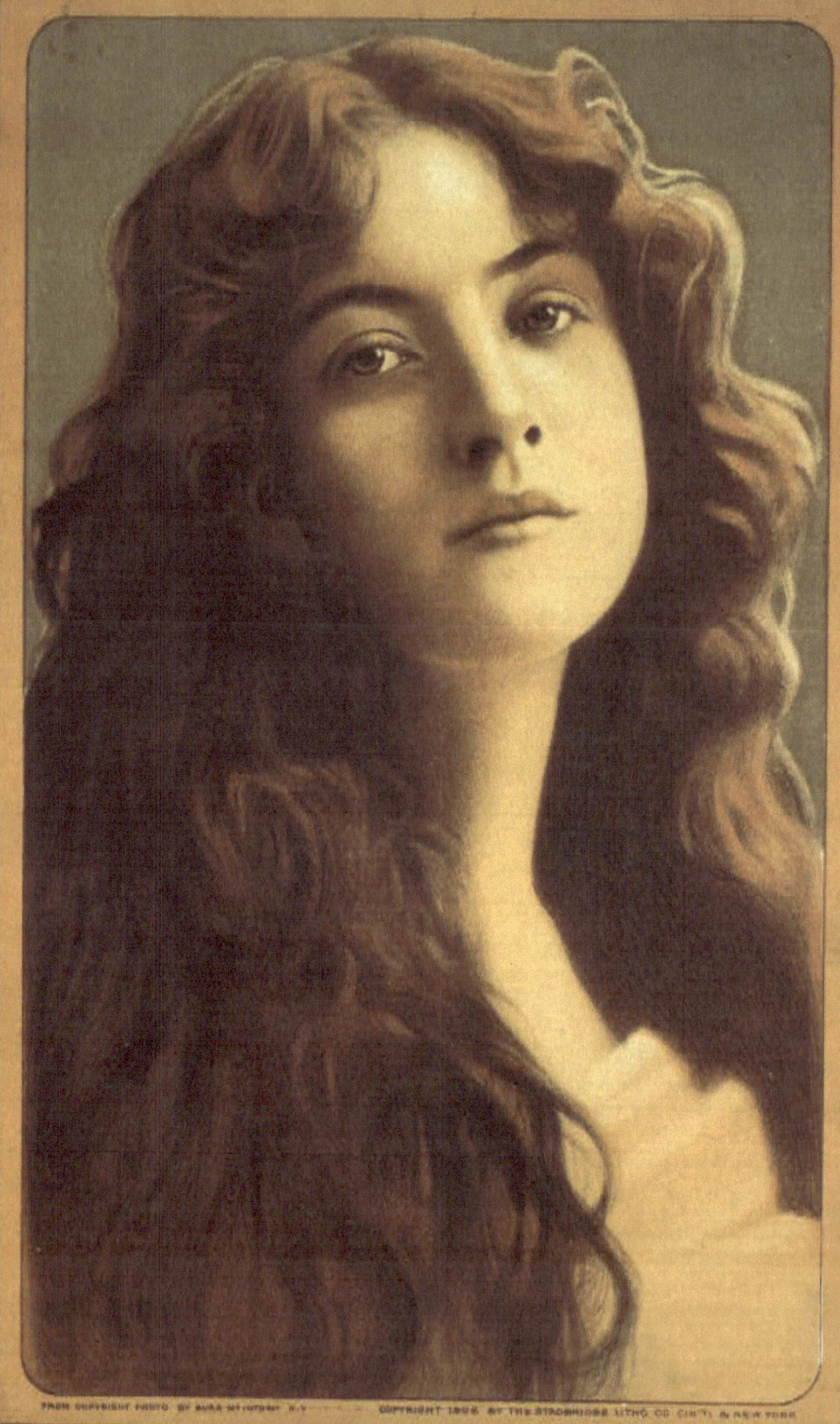

MAUDE FEALY

MANAGEMENT JOHN CORT

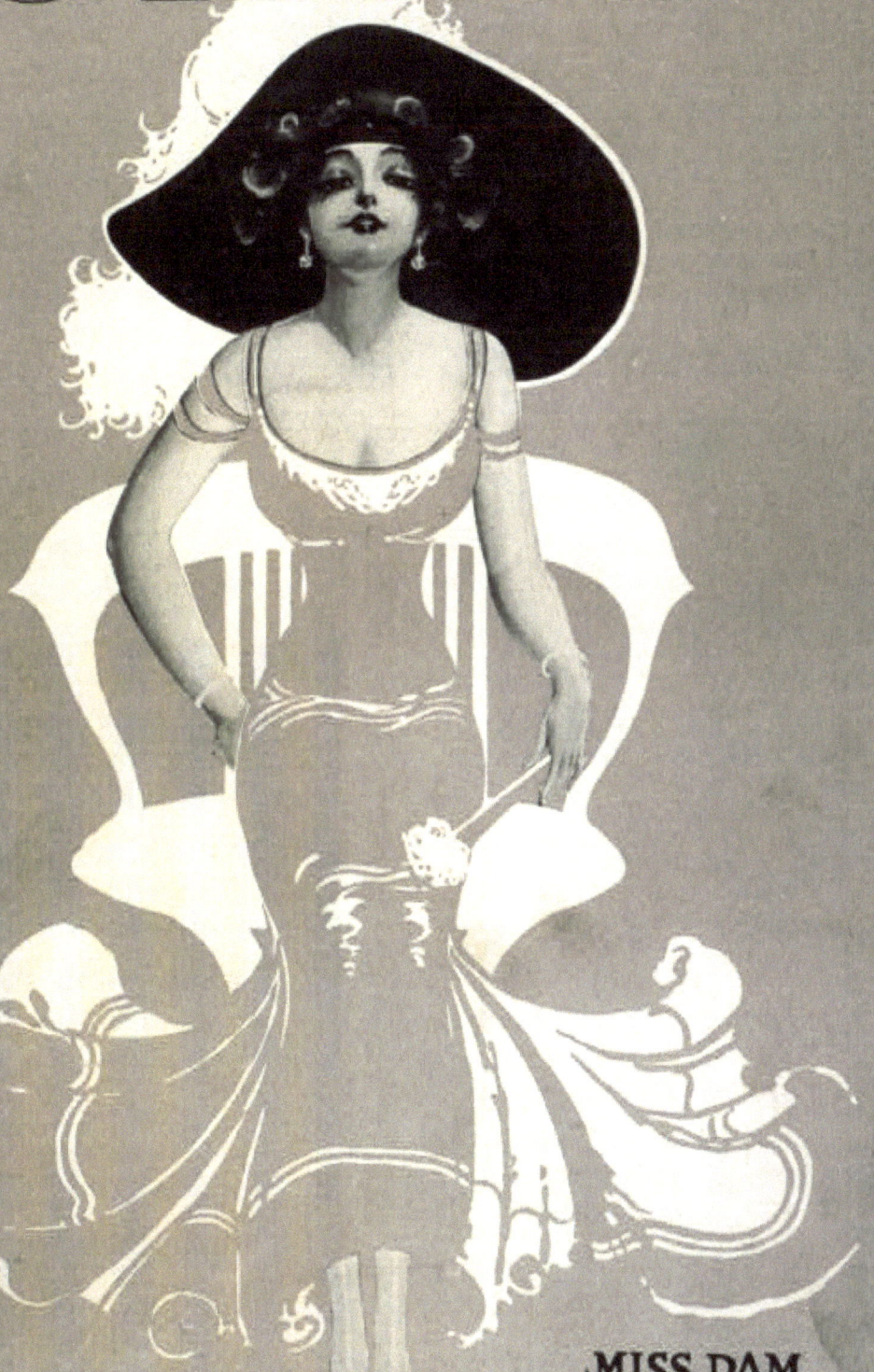

CLYDE FITCH'S
GREATEST COMEDY
"GIRLS"

MISS PAM

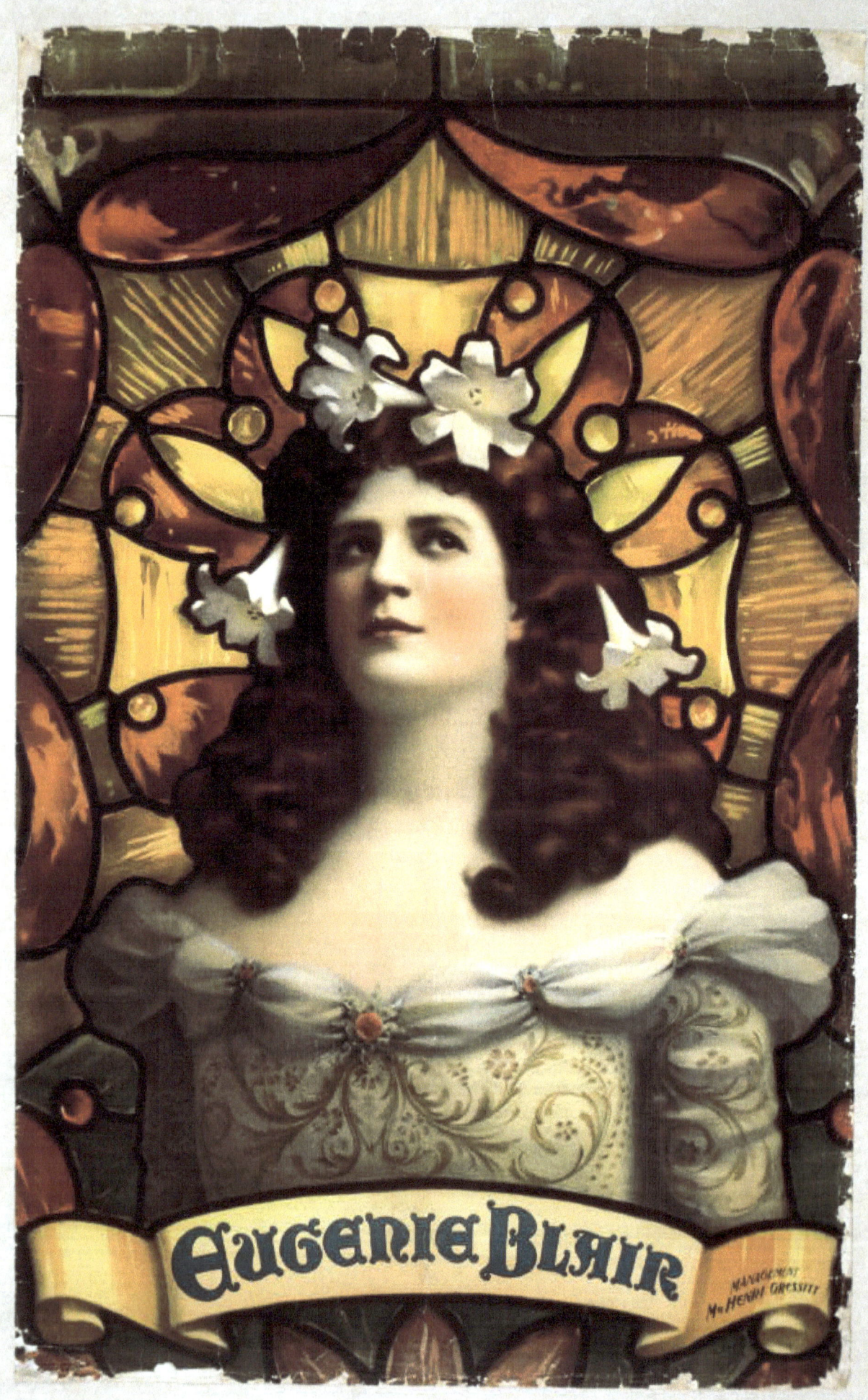

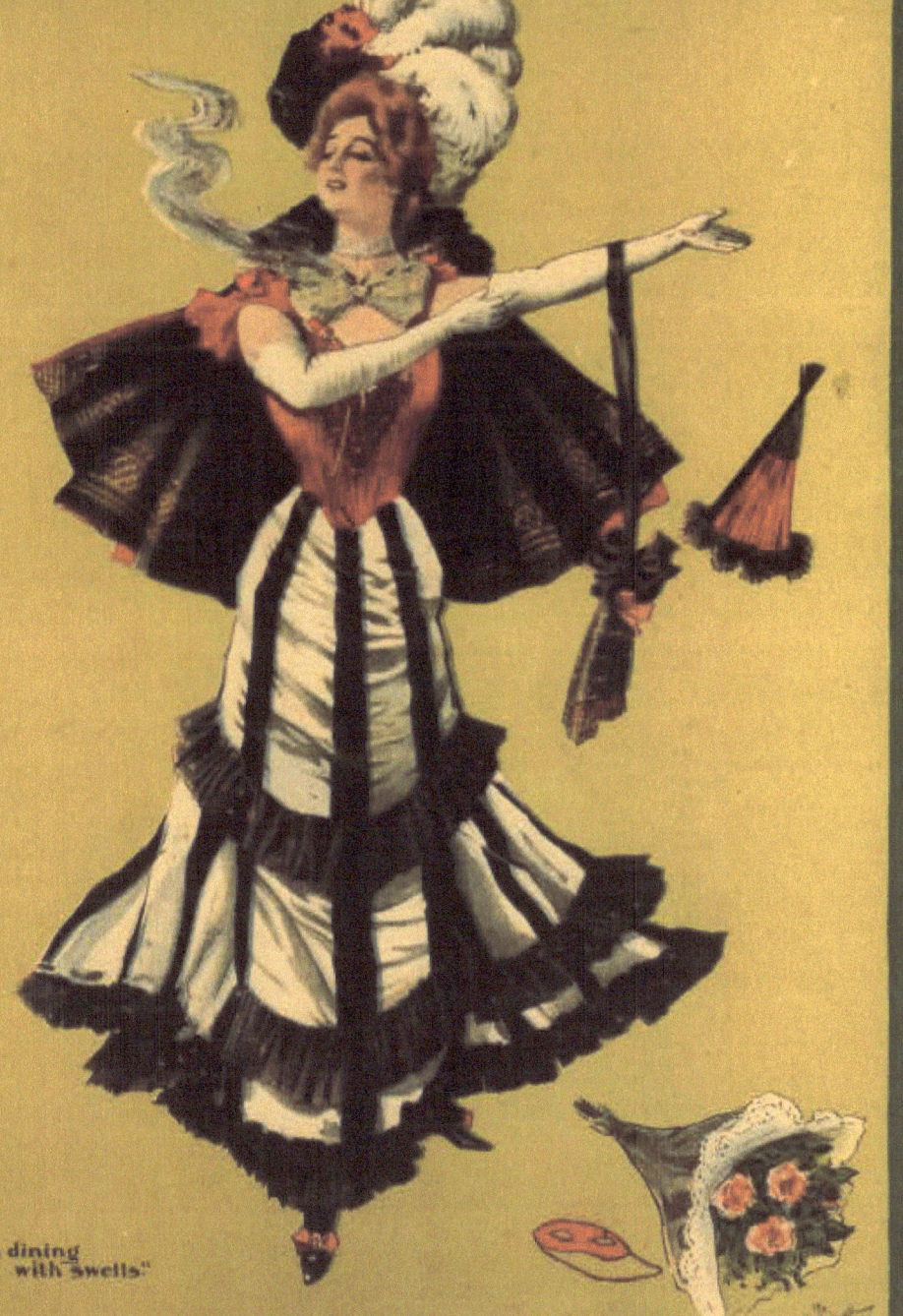

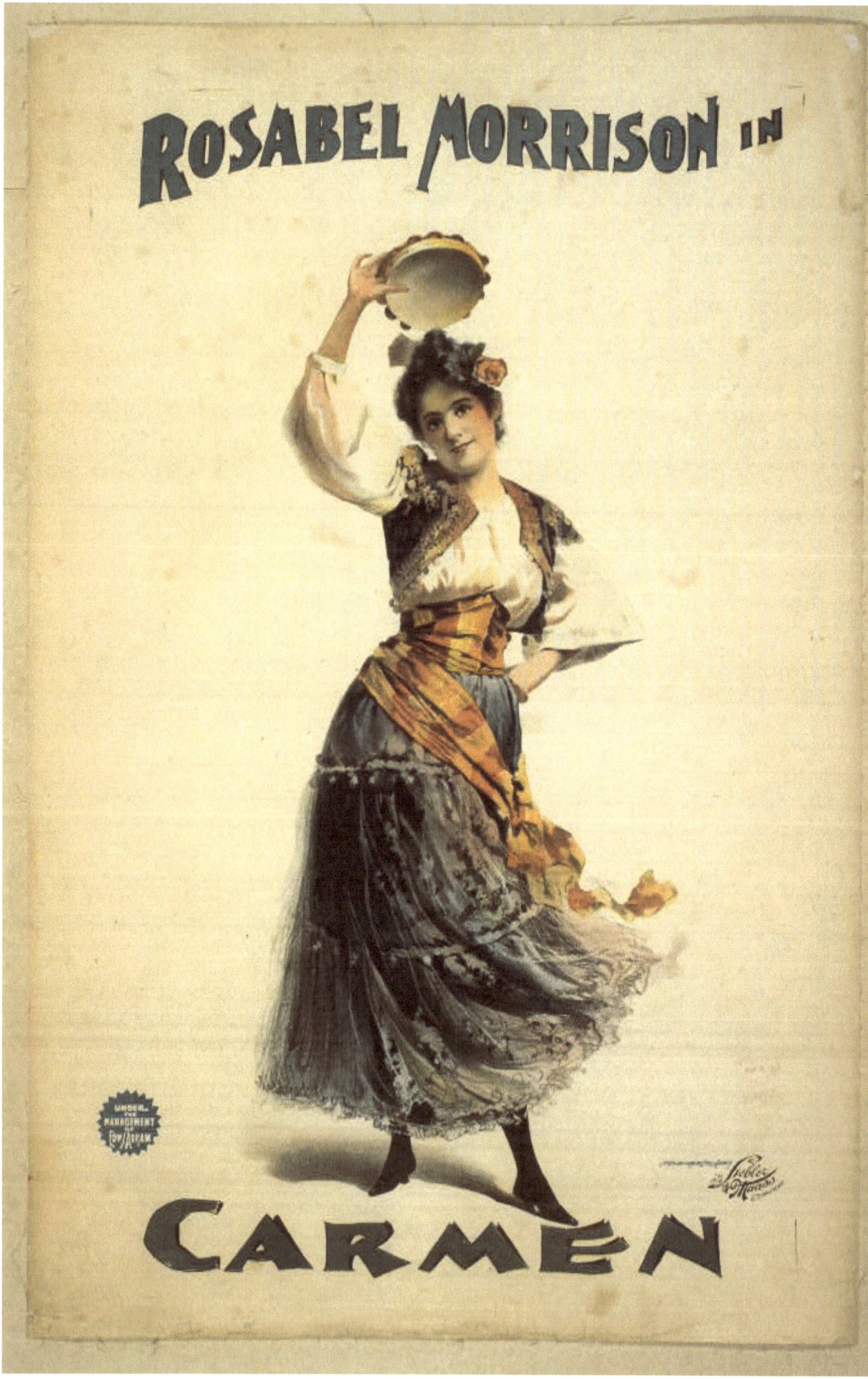

ROSABEL MORRISON IN

CARMEN

Selden's funny farce—
—A Spring Chicken

"THE DRESDEN DOLL"

Madeline—
Marshall—

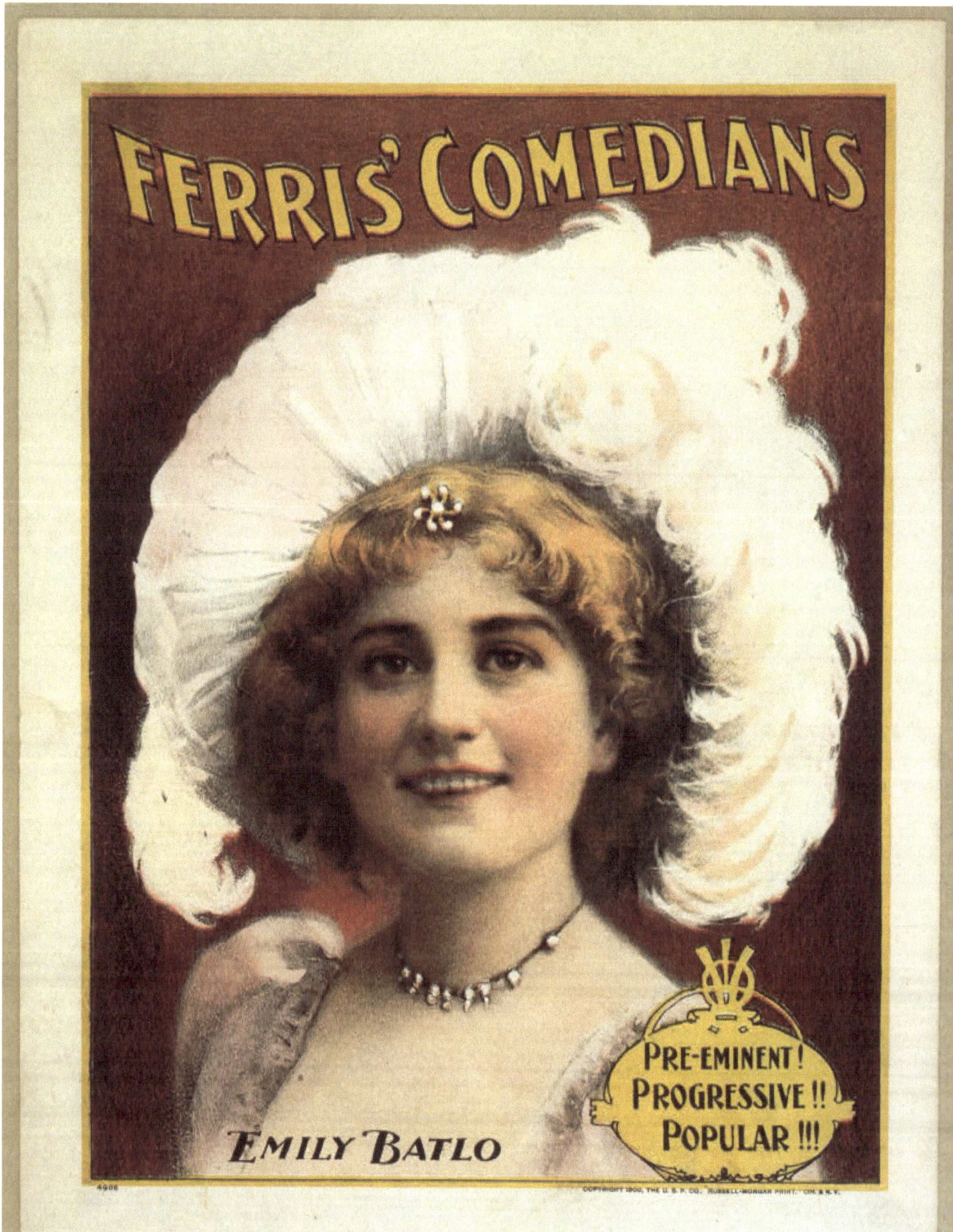
FERRIS' COMEDIANS
PRE-EMINENT!
PROGRESSIVE!!
POPULAR!!!
EMILY BATLO

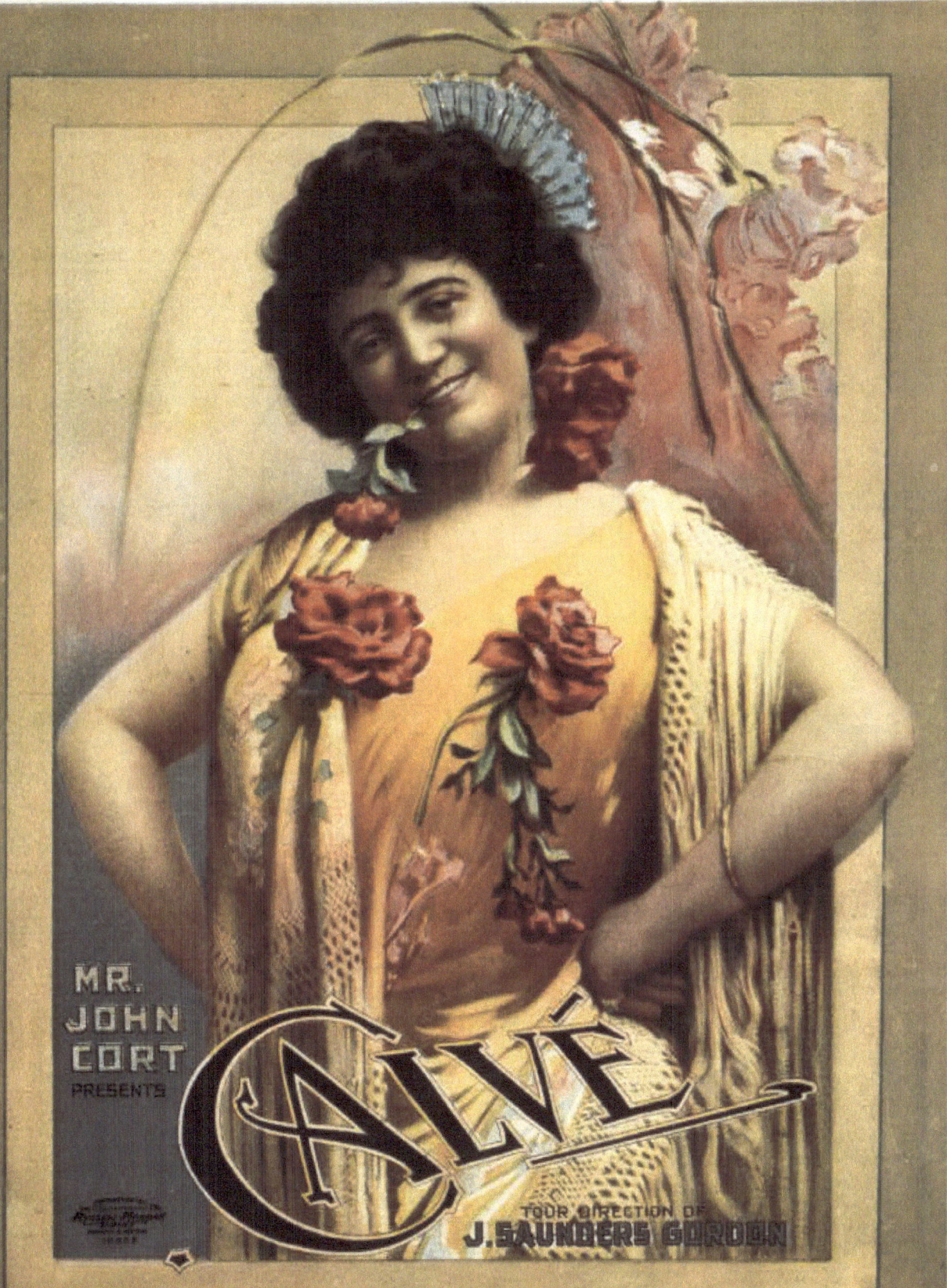

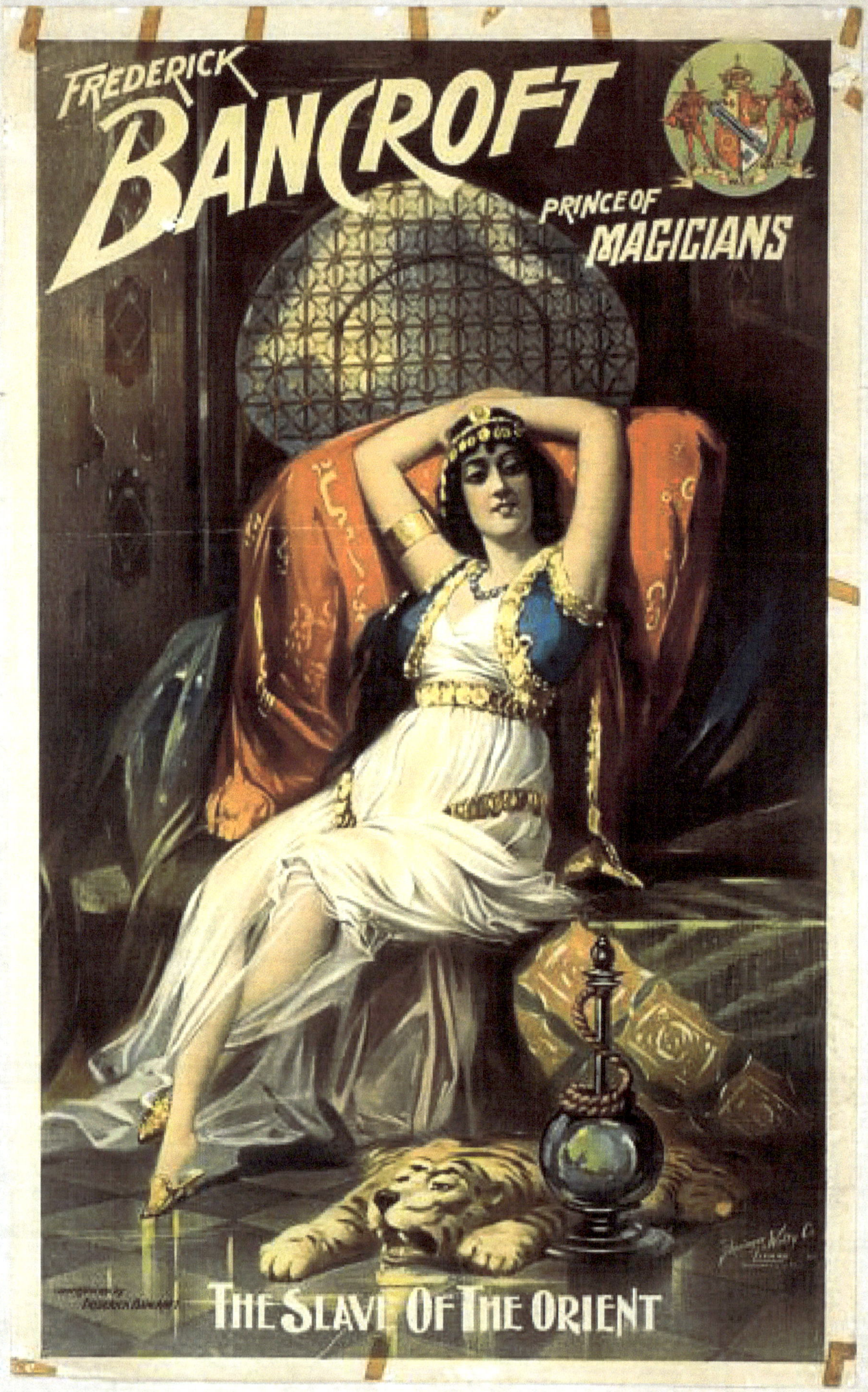
FREDERICK
BANCROFT
PRINCE OF
MAGICIANS
THE SLAVE OF THE ORIENT

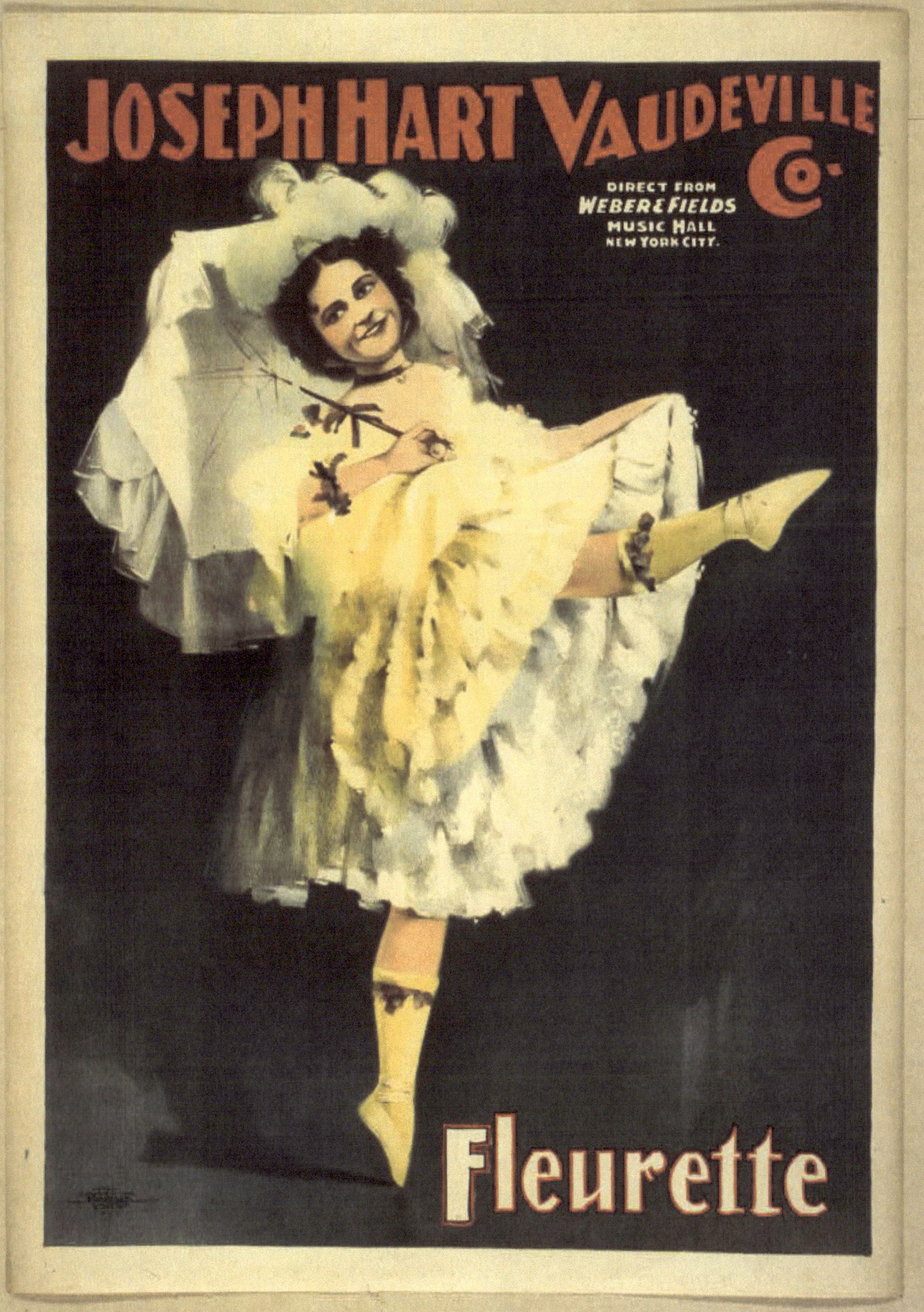
JOSEPH HART VAUDEVILLE
Co.
DIRECT FROM
WEBER & FIELDS
MUSIC HALL
NEW YORK CITY.
Fleurette

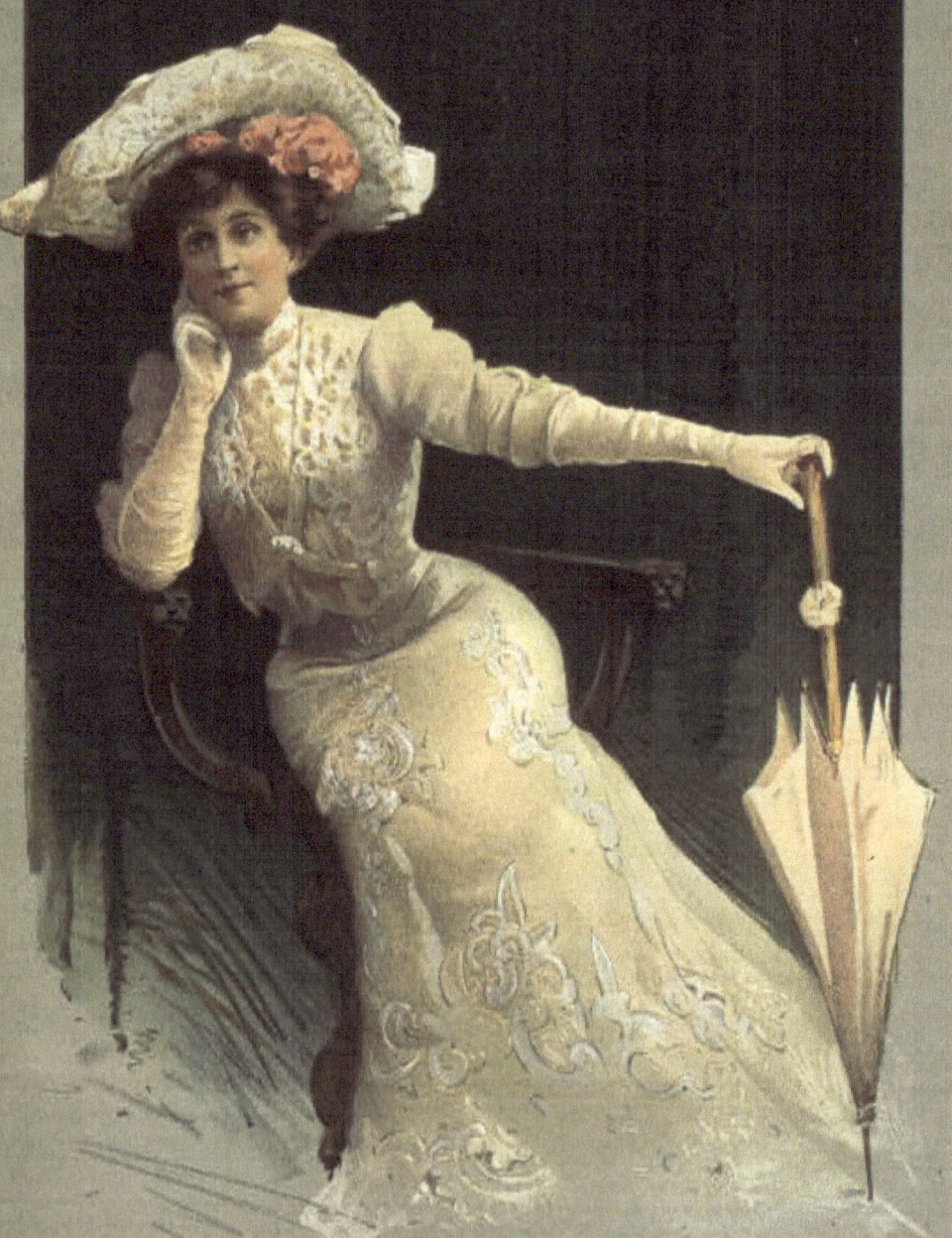

HURLY- EXTRAVAGANZA
BURLY AND REFINED VAUDEVILLE

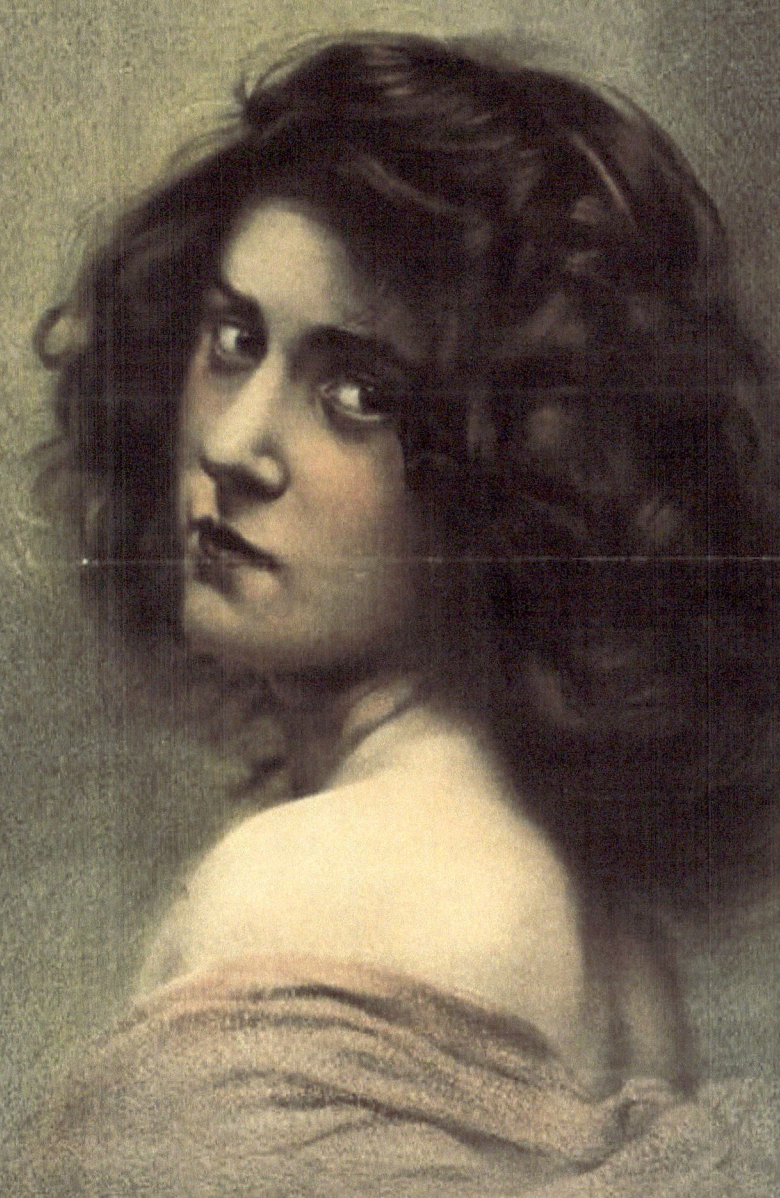

SADIE HARRIS
DANCER

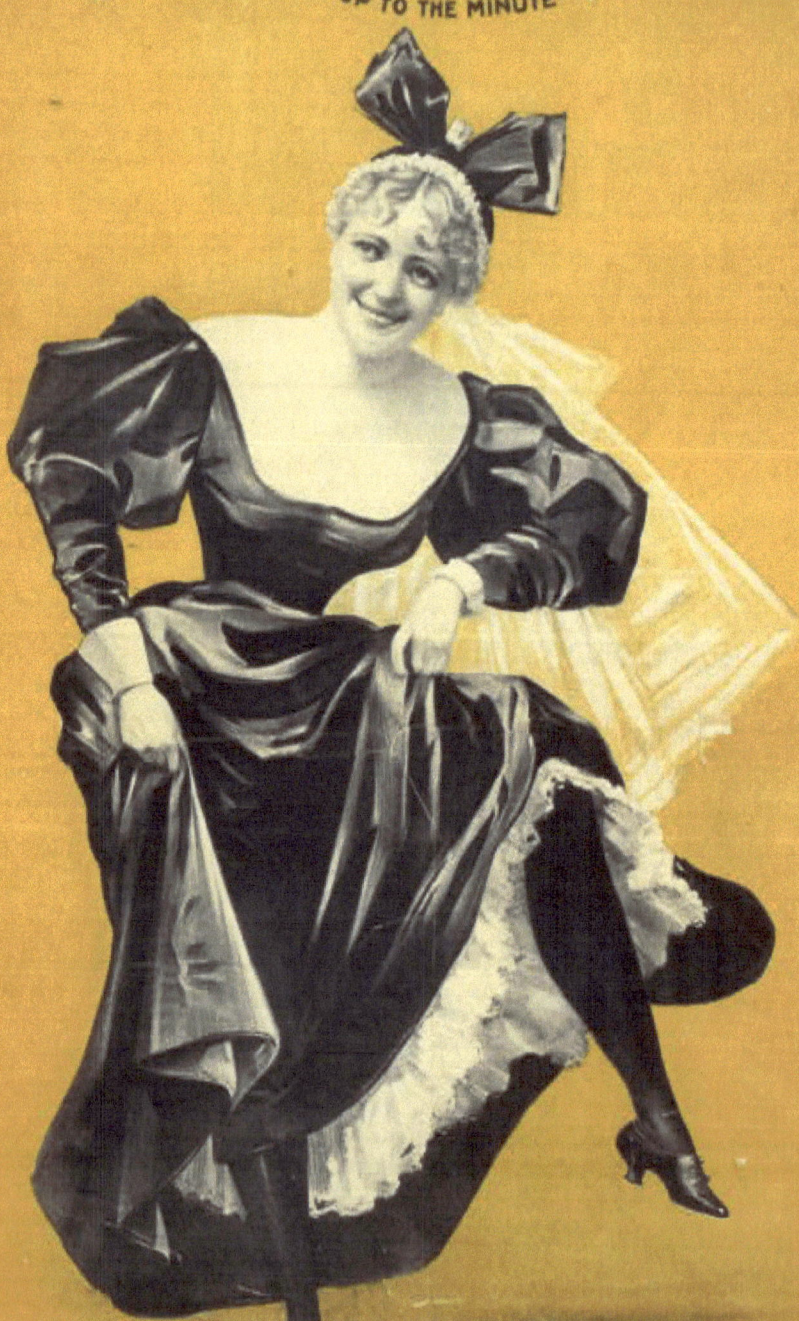

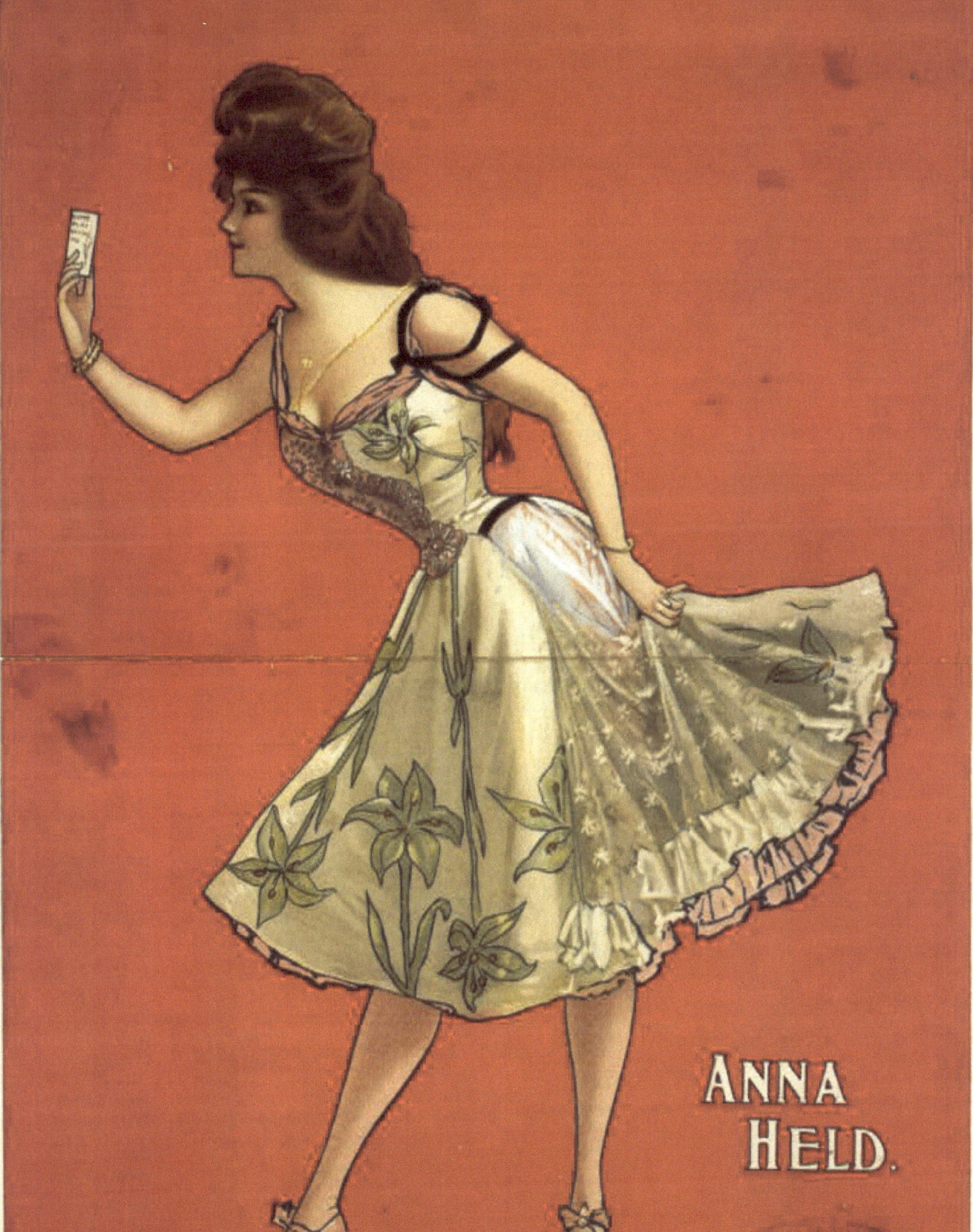

ANNA
HELD.

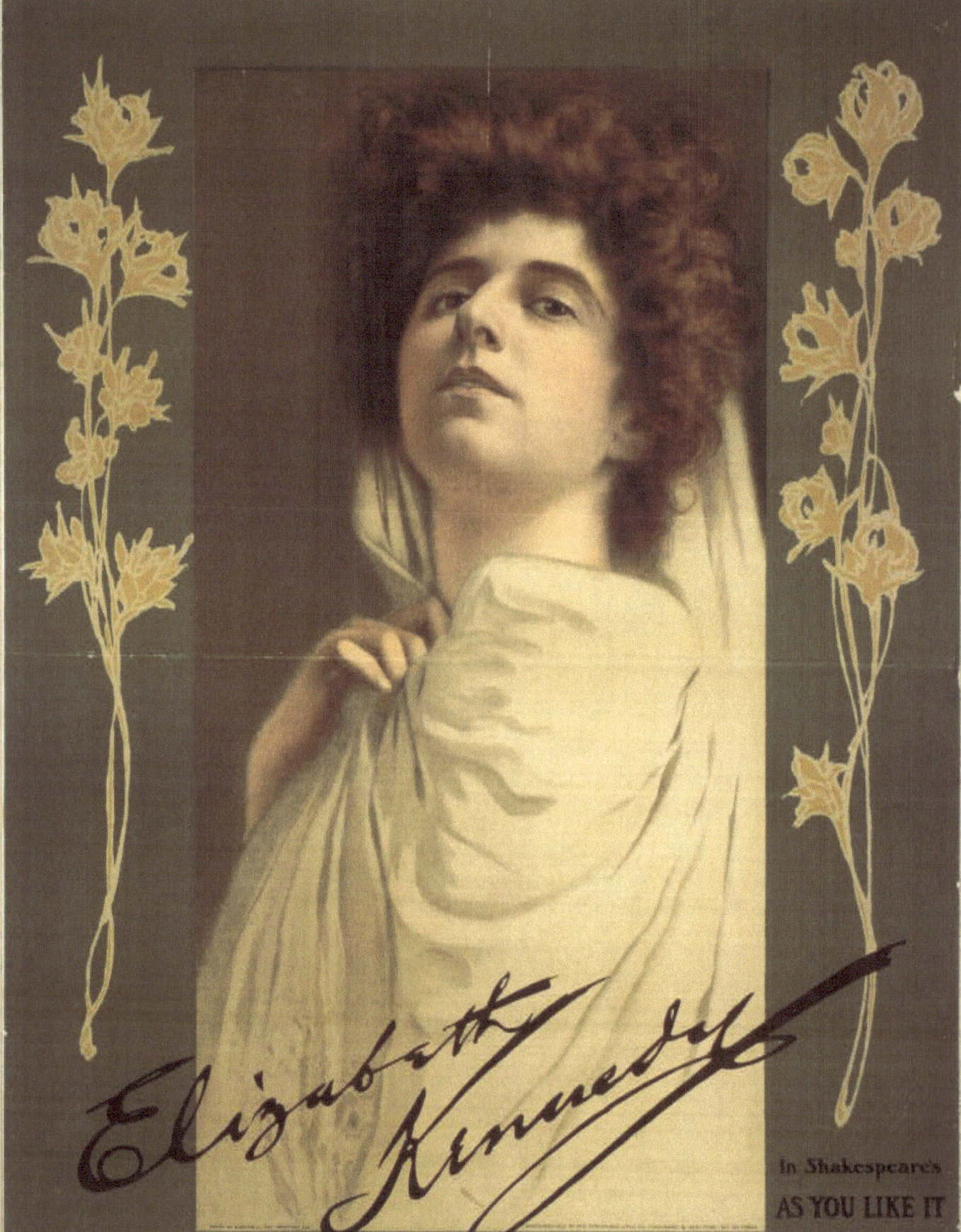

Elizabeth Kennedy

In Shakespeare's
AS YOU LIKE IT

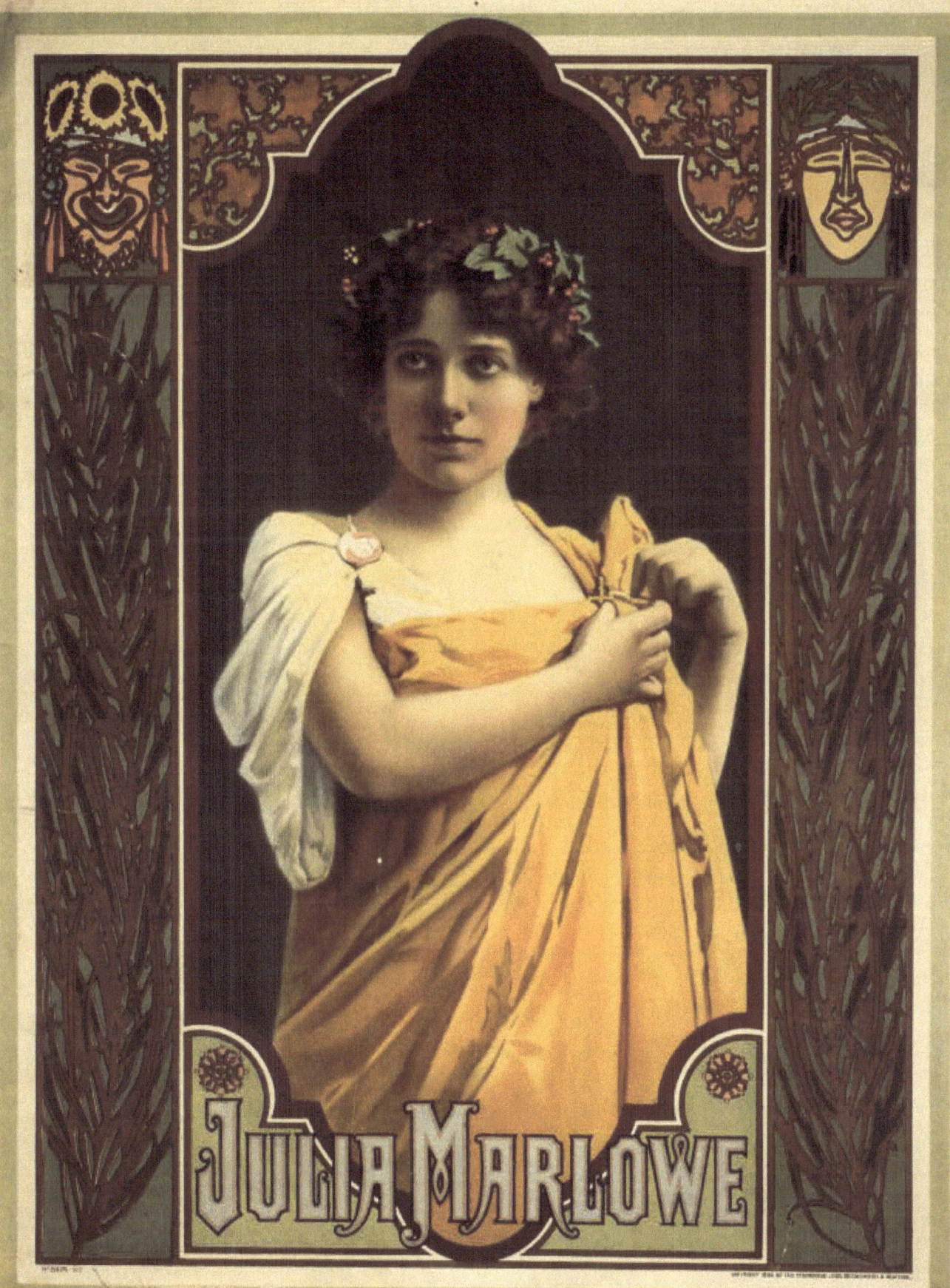

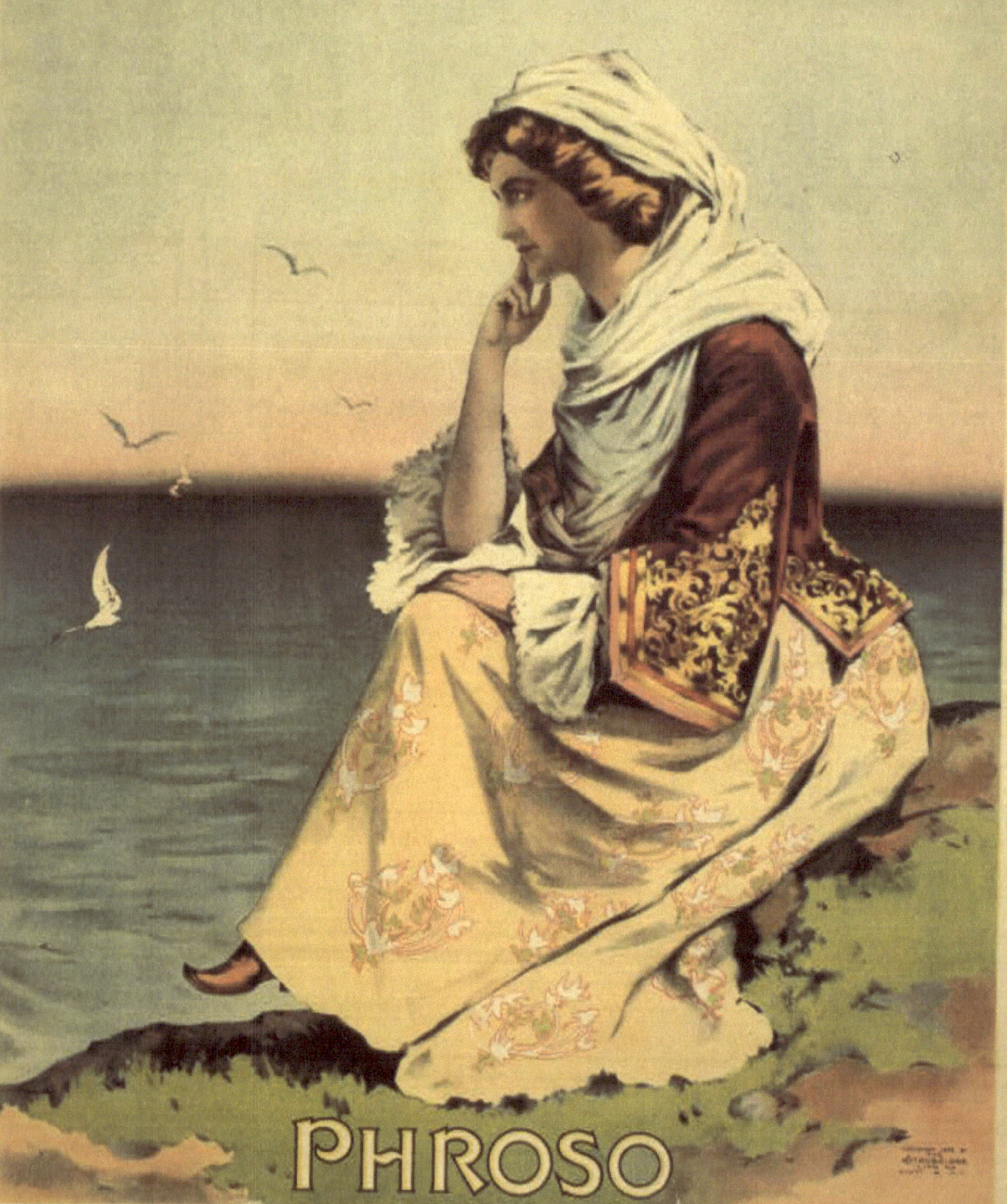

CHARLES FROHMAN PRESENTS A NEW PLAY BY ANTHONY HOPE

PHROSO

PHROSO

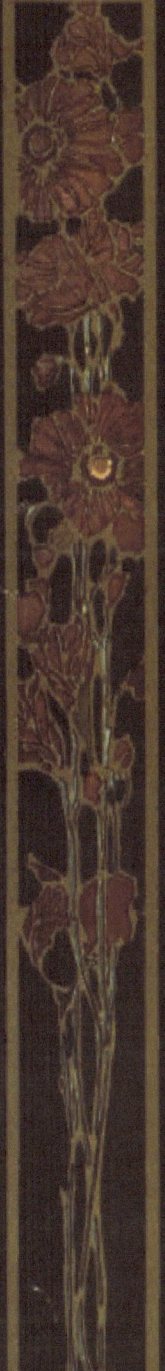
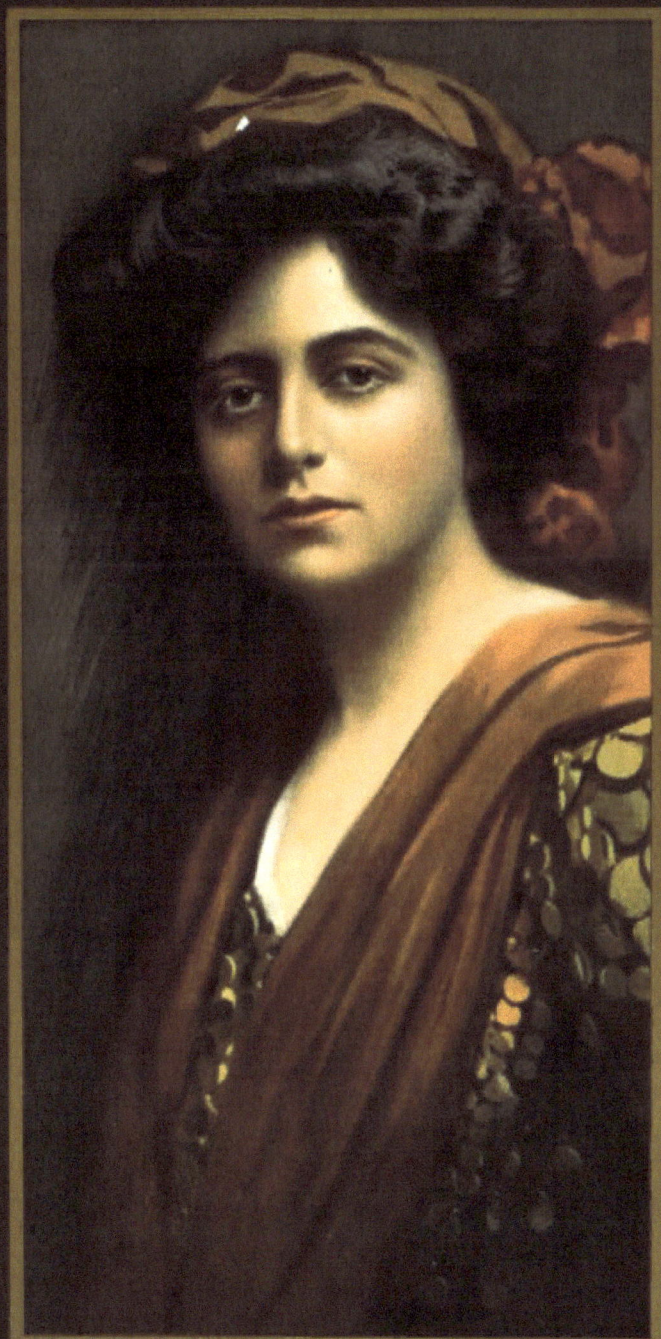
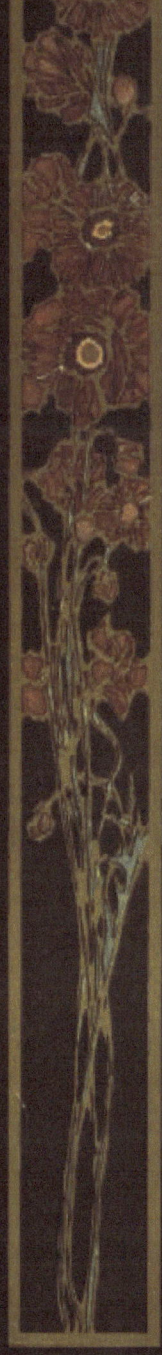

Miss MAXINE ELLIOTT

GEO. J. APPLETON Manager

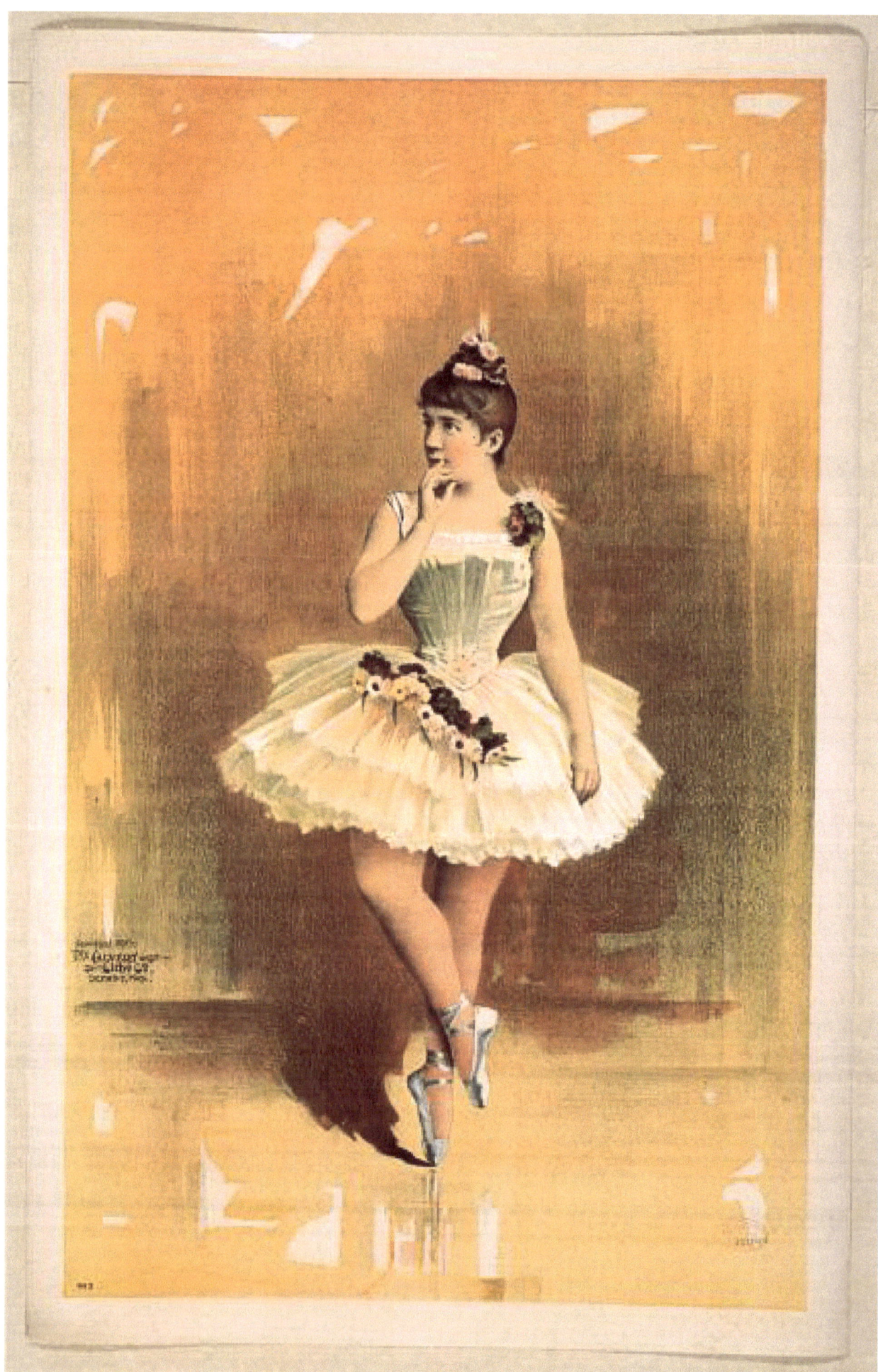

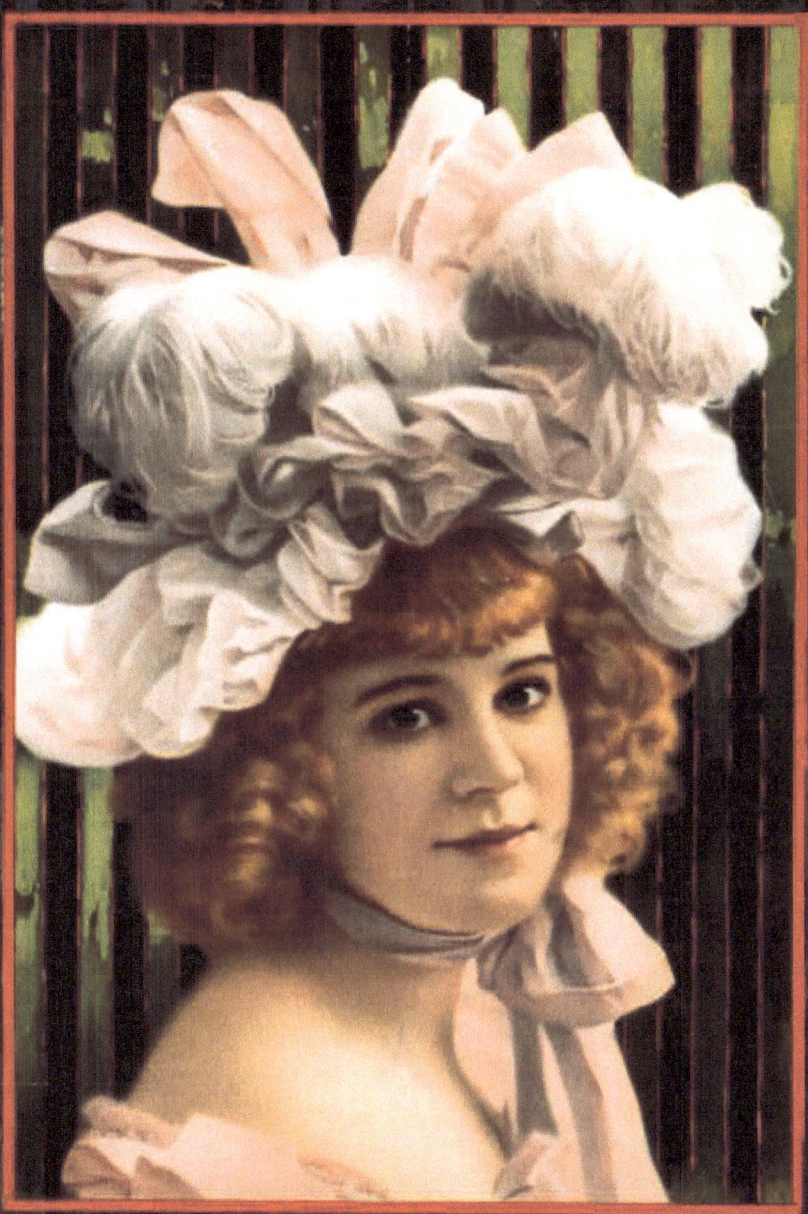

HOYT'S A BRASS MONKEY

MAZIE TRUMBULL

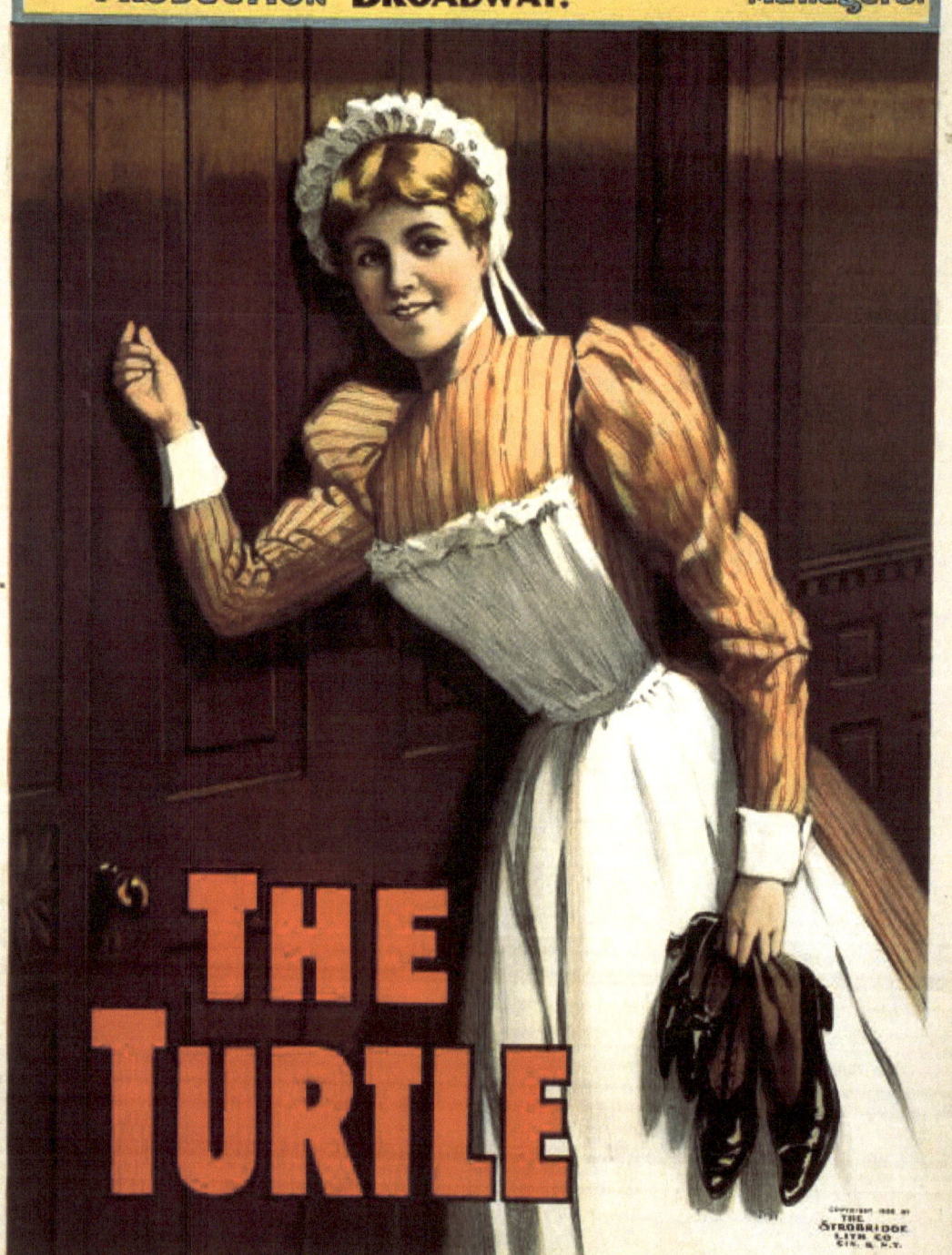

MANHATTAN THEATRE

F. ZIEGFELD Jr's PRODUCTION 33RD ST. AND BROADWAY. BRADY & ZIEGFELD Managers.

THE TURTLE

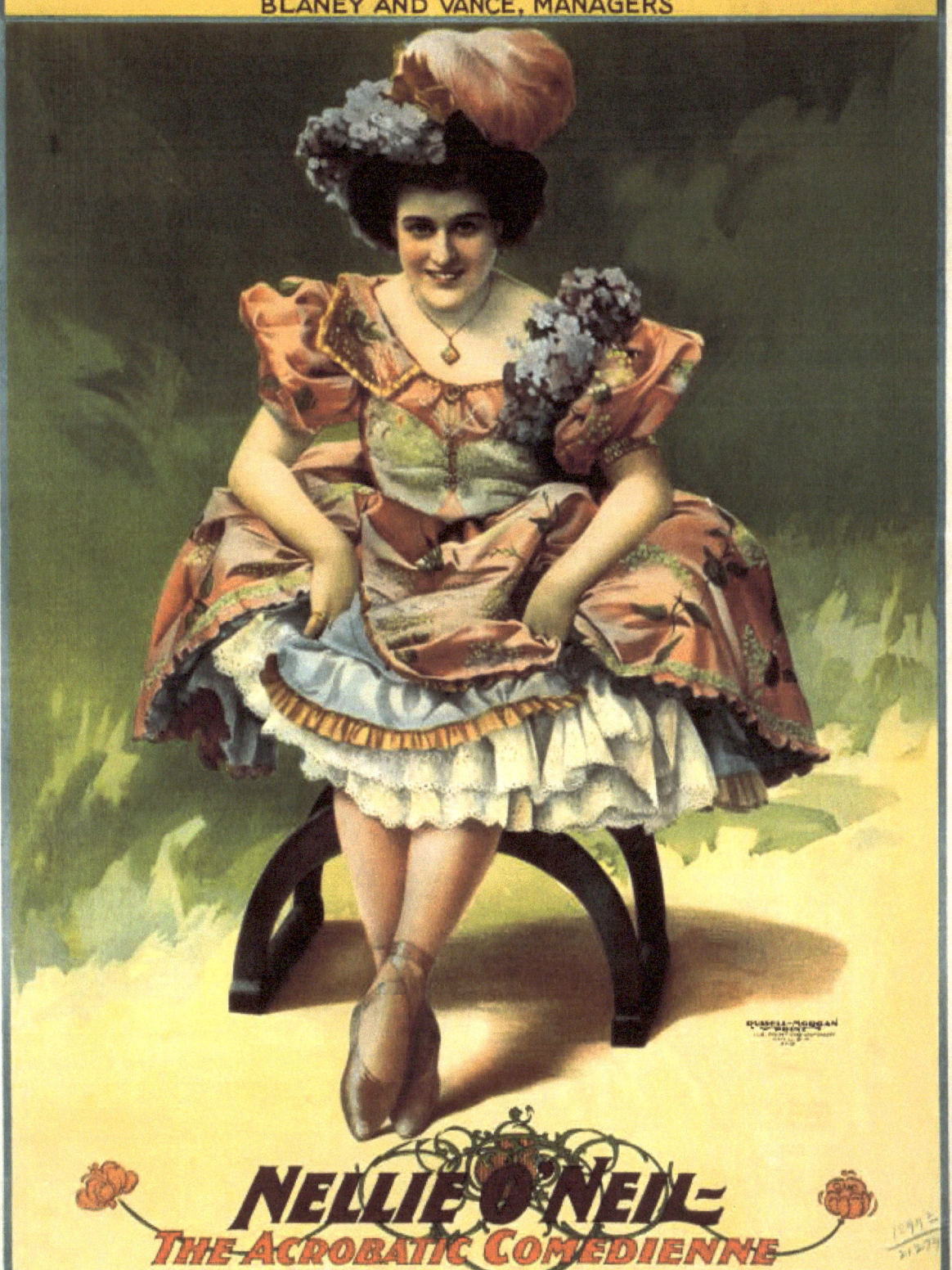

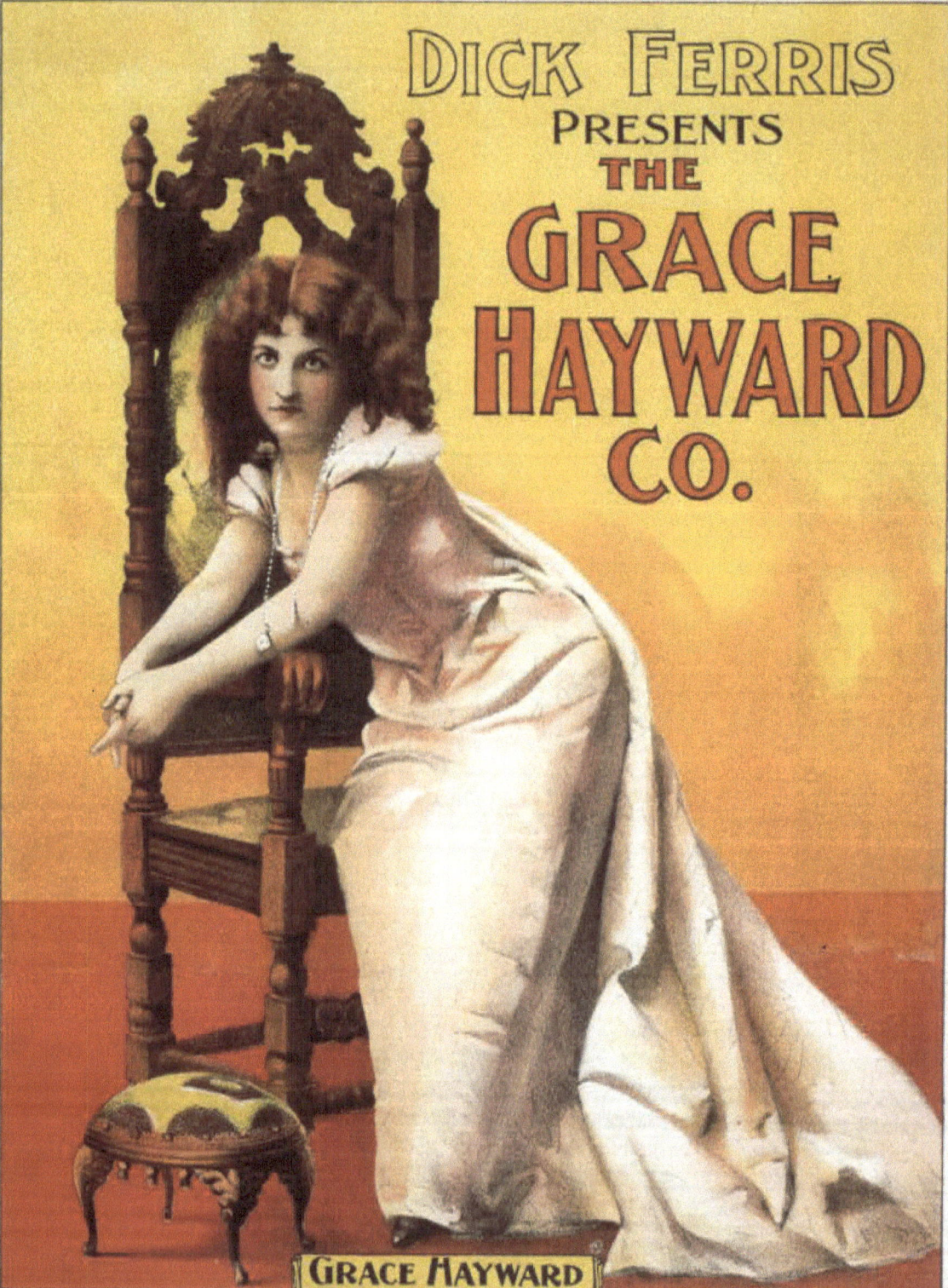

GRACE HAYWARD

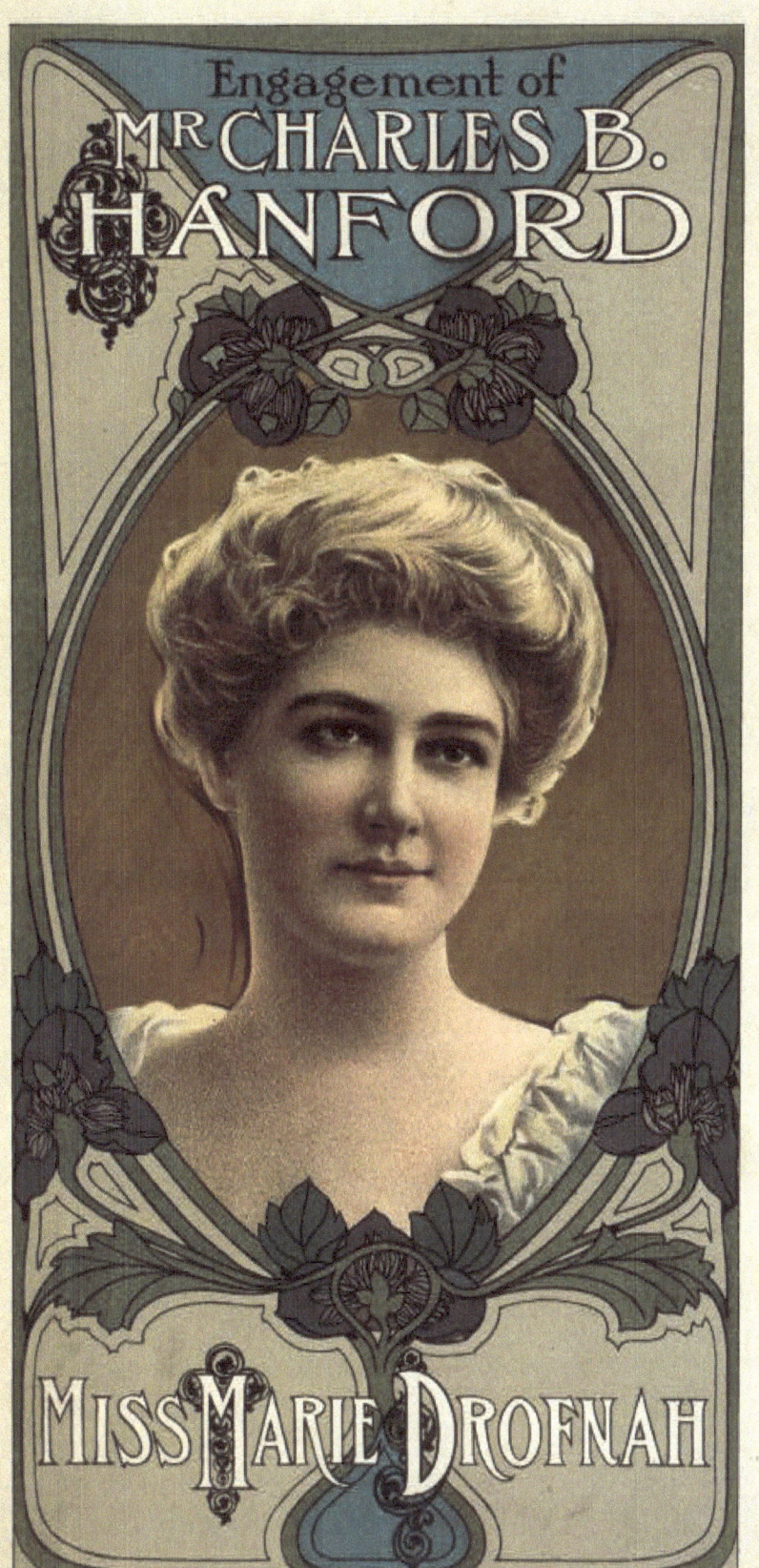

Engagement of

Mr CHARLES B. HANFORD

MISS MARIE DROFNAH

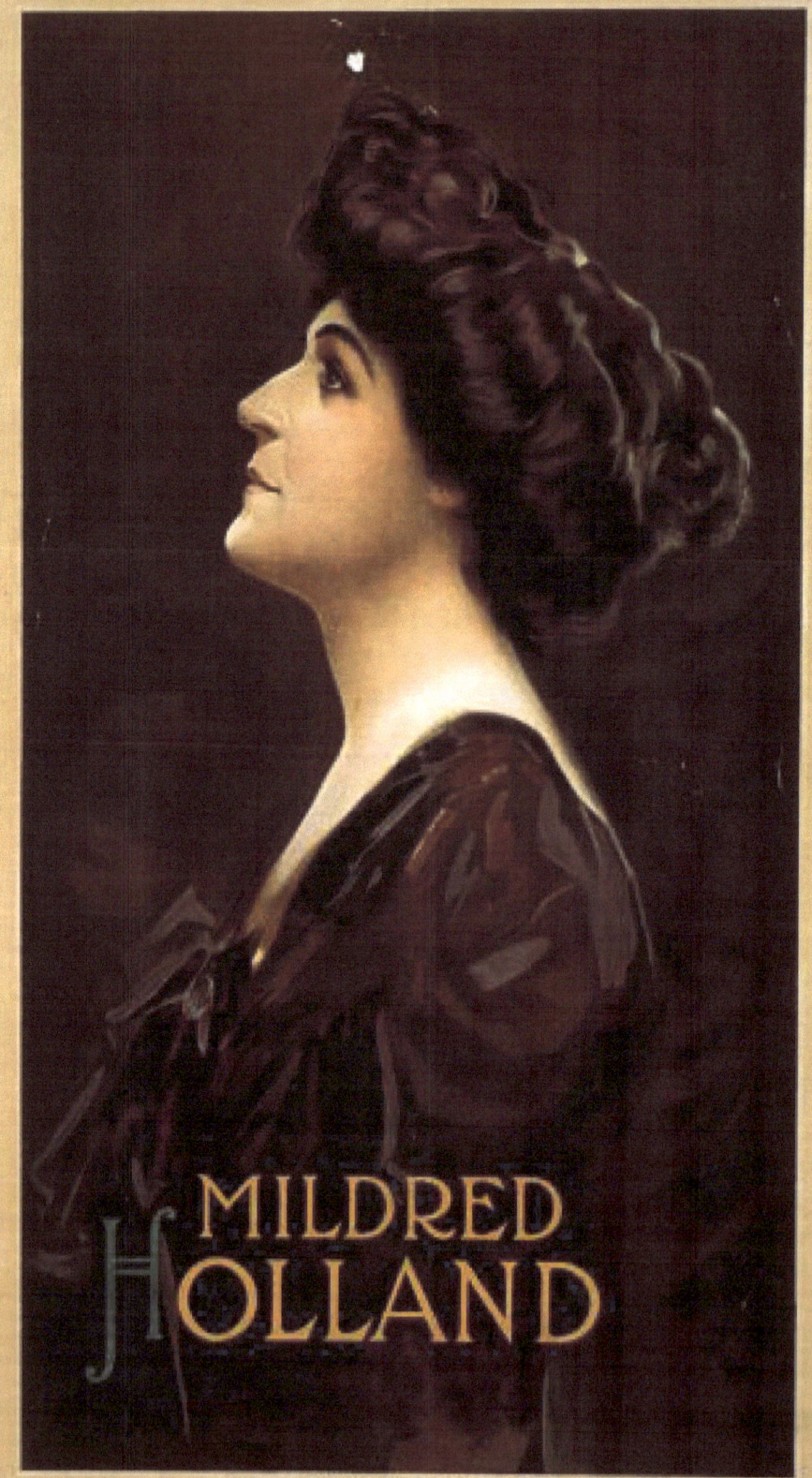

MILDRED HOLLAND

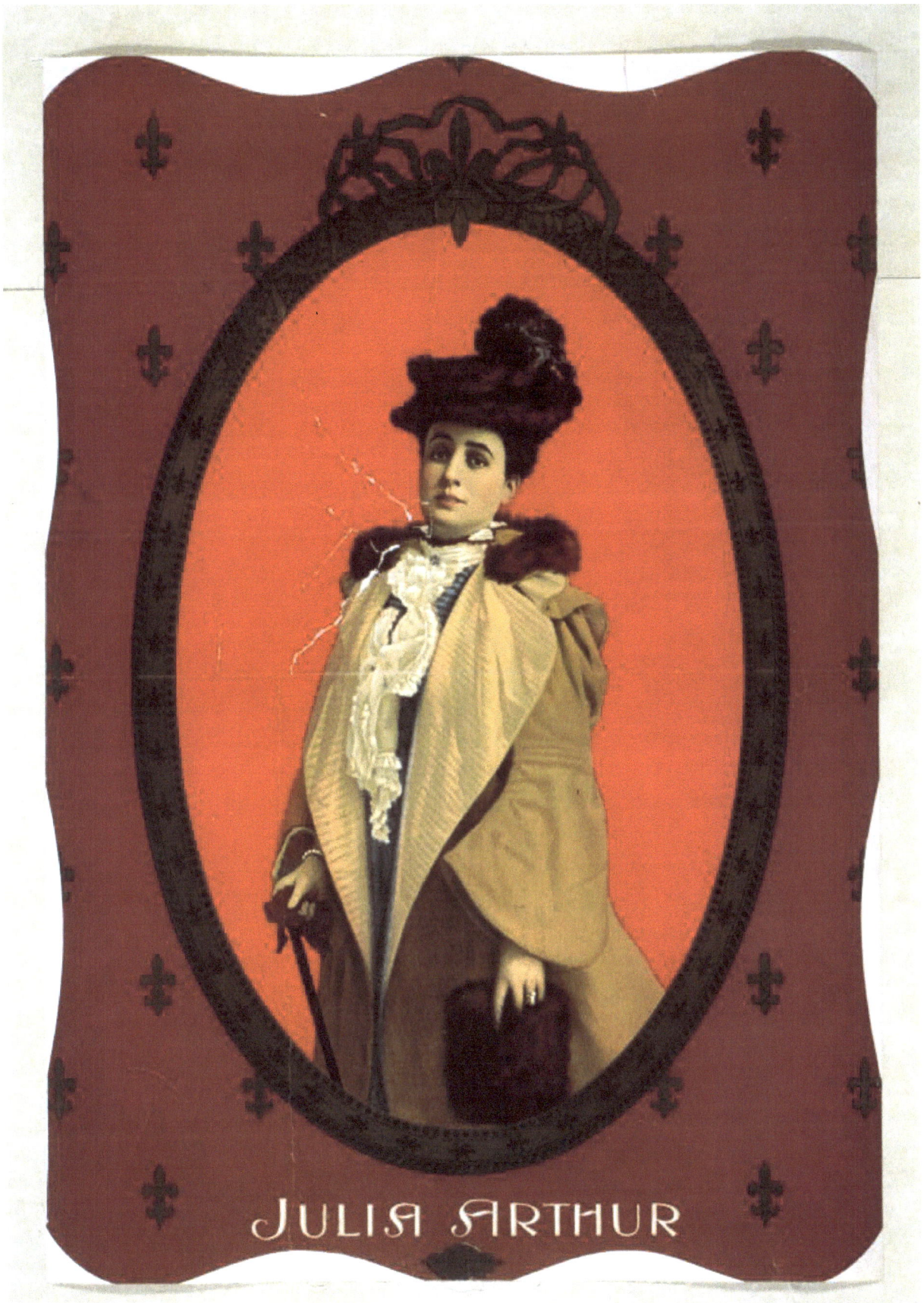

JULIA ARTHUR

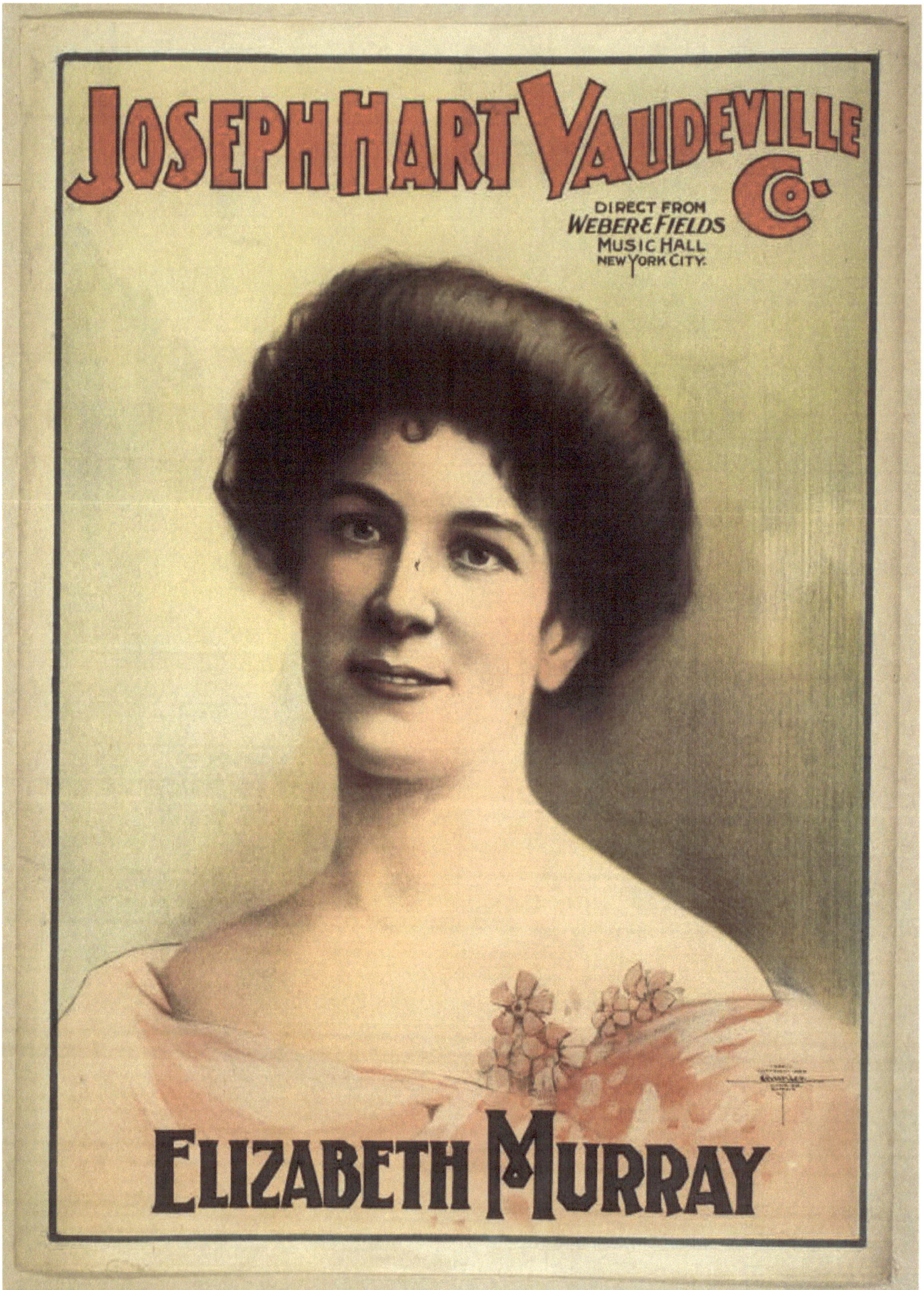
JOSEPH HART VAUDEVILLE Co.
DIRECT FROM
WEBER & FIELDS
MUSIC HALL
NEW YORK CITY.
ELIZABETH MURRAY

GEORGE BARR McCUTCHEON'S

Beverly

DIRECTION
A. G. DELAMATER
AND
WILLIAM NORRIS (INC.)

DRAMATIZED FROM
THE NOVEL BY
ROB'T. M. BAKER

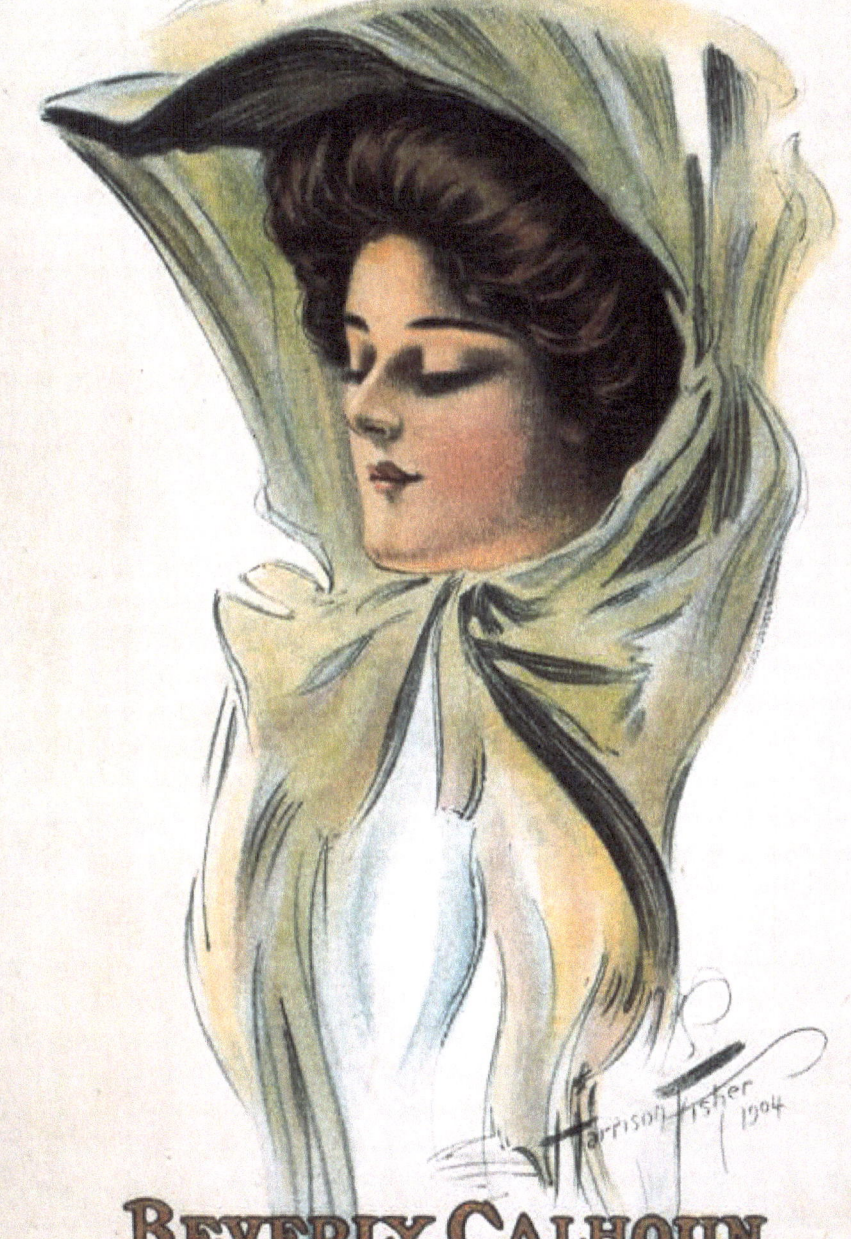

BEVERLY CALHOUN

"Devils Auction"
1920.

Plate-W-1401

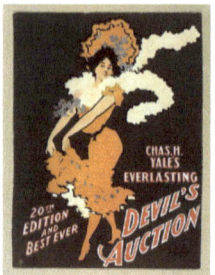

"The Princess Chic"
1900.

Plate-W-1402

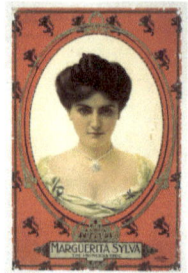

"Miss Maxine Elliott"
1905

Plate-W-1403

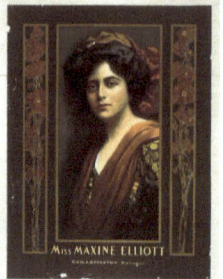

"Elizabeth Kennedy in
Shakespeare's As You Like
It"
1903.

Plate-W-1404

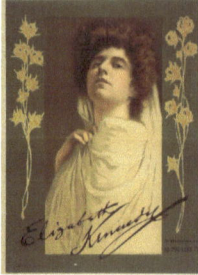

"Sapho New York's Raging
Sensation"
1900.

Plate-W-1405

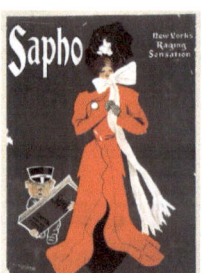

"Sweely, Shipman & Co.
Present The Duchess of
Devonshire"
1906.
Plate-W-1406

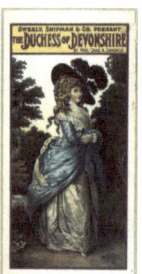

"Maude Fealy"
1906

Plate-W-1407

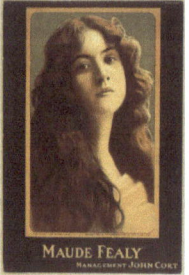

"Girls"
1910

Plate-W-1408

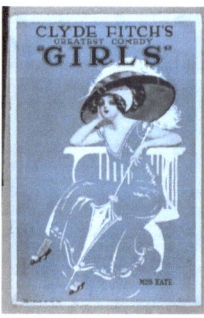

"Girls"
1910

Plate-W-1409

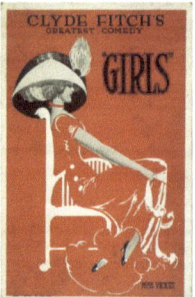

"Girls"
1910

Plate-W-1410

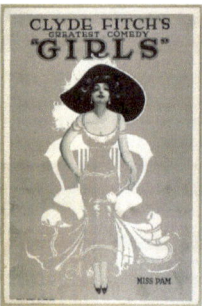

"Nellie McHenry in A Night At the Circus by H. Grattan Donnelly"
1893
Plate-W-1411

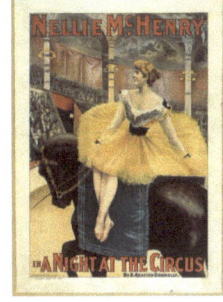

"Eugenie Blair"
1899

Plate-W-1412

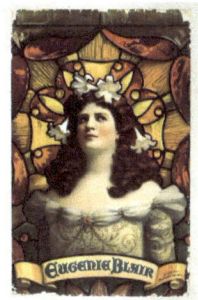

"Rosabel Morrison in Carmen"
1896

Plate-W-1413

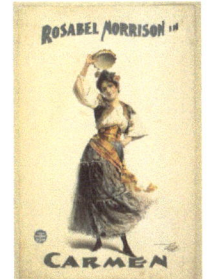

"Silver Spur"
1887

Plate-W-1414

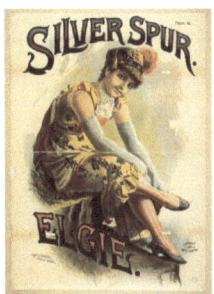

"Ferris' Comedians"
1900

Plate-W-1415

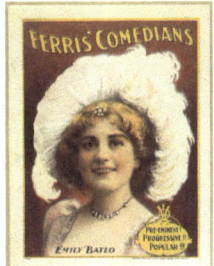

"Mr. John Cort Presents Calve"
1907

Plate-W-1416

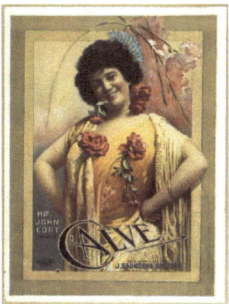

"Frederick Bancroft, Prince of Magicians"
1895

Plate-W-1417

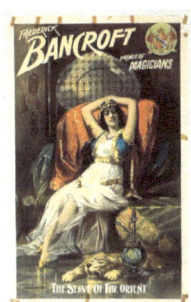

"Joseph Hard Vaudeville Co. Direct from Weber & Fields Music Hall, New York City"
1899
Plate-W-1418

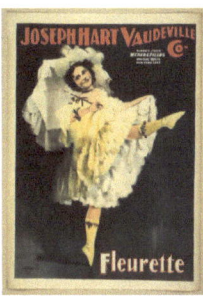

"The Emotional Actress, Alberta Gallatin"
1906

Plate-W-1419

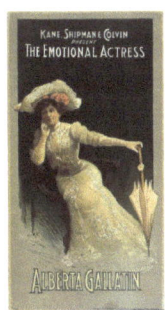

"Hurly-Burly Extravaganza and Refined Vaudeville"
1899

Plate-W-1420

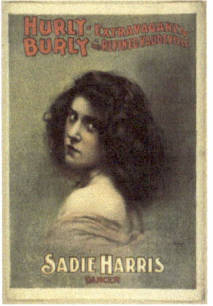

"Weber's Parisian Widows
Up to the Minute"
1897

Plate-W-1421

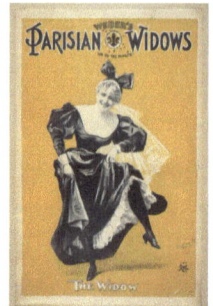

"Anna Held"
1899

Plate-W-1422

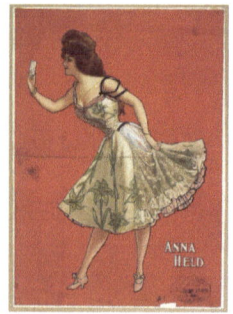

"Henri Gressit Presents
Eugenie Blair in David
Belasco's Great Play,
Zaza"
1903
Plate-W-1423

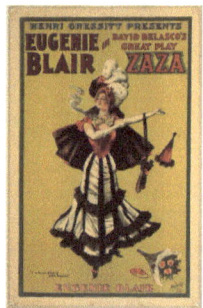

"Julia Marlowe"
1899

Plate-W-1424

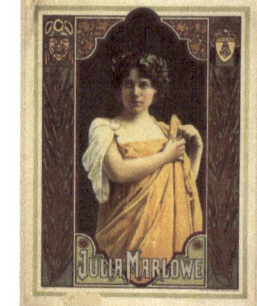

"Phroso by Anthony
Hope"
1898

Plate-W-1425

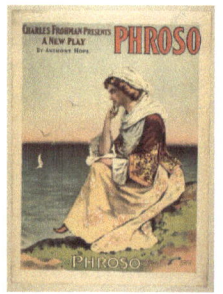

"Selden's Funny Farce, A
Spring Chicken"
1898

Plate-W-1426

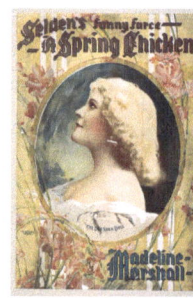

"Ballerina in White
Costume with Flowers in
Dance Pose"
1890

Plate-W-1427

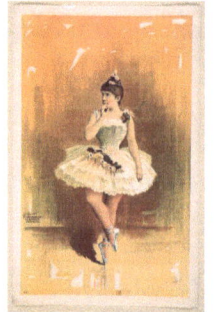

"Hoyt's A Brass Monkey"
1900.

Plate-W-1428

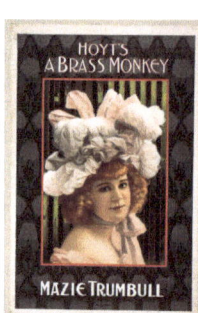

"The Turtle F. Ziegfeld Jr's
Production"
1898

Plate-W-1429

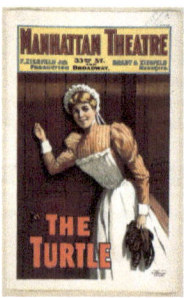

"Chas. E. Blaney's Big
Extravaganze Success, A
Female Drummer"
1899

Plate-W-1430

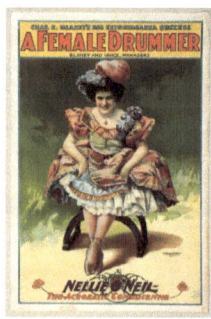

"Dick Ferris Presents the
Grace Hayward Co."
1900

Plate-W-1431

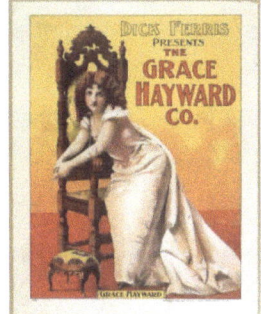

"Engagement of Mr.
Charles B. Hanford"
1906

Plate-W-1432

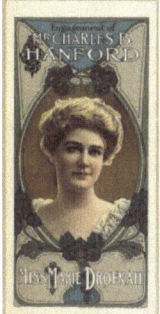

"Mildred Holland"
1908

Plate-W-1433

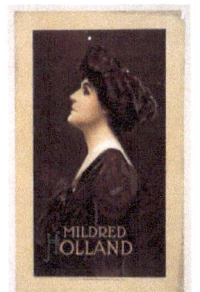

"Julia Arthur"
1899

Plate-W-1434

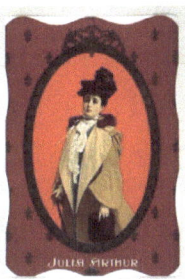

"Elizabeth Murray"
1899

Plate-W-1435

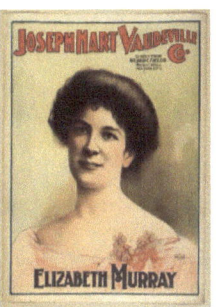

"Beverly"
1904

Plate-W-1436

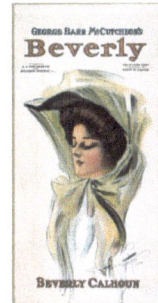

To Order Posters and Inquire about Sizes and Prices:

Email Poster Number (Plate-W-14XX) to
manager@worldgreatart.com

World Great Art™ Publishing

www.WorldGreatArt.com

2013